Praise for *Citizen Capitalism*

"This book offers a transformative plan to make corporate ownership and governance more inclusive. It attempts to harness corporate power and resources in the tackling of the challenges of poverty and empowerment. At the heart of the book is the relationship between corporations and society. Through their proposal, the authors strive for a synergic relationship benefiting society. With clinical precision and an extraordinary grasp of history, the book offers a brilliant diagnosis of critical issues facing the world in the field of corporate governance. This is an important and valuable book. It reminds us that the only legitimate end of corporate governance is the well-being of society."

—Muna Ndulo, Professor of Law; Elizabeth and Arthur Reich Director, Leo and Arvilla Berger International Legal Studies Program; and Director, Institute for African Development, Cornell University

"Corporations—like governments—play an essential role in the lives of every American. But most Americans have an extremely limited ability to influence corporate decision-making, and we all live with the consequences. Stout, Gramitto, and Belinfanti offer a bold and creative alternative: What if we had a tool that gave every American a say in how corporations are run—like a superpowered pension fund that made corporations accountable to more than the bottom line? This is a powerful and timely idea, and *Citizen Capitalism* makes the case extraordinarily well."

—Deborah N. Archer, Associate Professor of Clinical Law, New York University School of Law

"The very bold plan to democratize corporate governance detailed by Stout, Gramitto, and Belinfanti in *Citizen Capitalism* is sure to be controversial in some circles, but it will also catalyze long-overdue discussions about the role of business in our society. Read this book."

—Alice Korngold, Author of *A Better World, Inc.*, and President and CEO, Korngold Consulting, LLC

D1495289

Citizen Capitalism

Other Books by Lynn Stout

The Shareholder Value Myth

Cultivating Conscience

(Princeton University Press, 2010, 978-0691-13995-1)

Citizen Capitalism

How a Universal Fund Can Provide Influence and Income to All

Lynn Stout

Sergio Gramitto

Tamara Belinfanti

Berrett–Koehler Publishers, Inc.
a BK Currents book

Berrett-Koehler Publishers, Inc.
1333 Broadway, Suite 1000
Oakland, CA 94612-1921
Tel: (510) 817-2277
Fax: (510) 817-2278
www.bkconnection.com

ORDERING INFORMATION

Quantity sales. Special discounts are available on quantity purchases by corporations, associations, and others. For details, contact the "Special Sales Department" at the Berrett-Koehler address above.

Individual sales. Berrett-Koehler publications are available through most bookstores. They can also be ordered directly from Berrett-Koehler:
Tel: (800) 929-2929; Fax: (802) 864-7626; www.bkconnection.com.

Orders for college textbook / course adoption use. Please contact Berrett-Koehler:
Tel: (800) 929-2929; Fax: (802) 864-7626.

Distributed to the U.S. trade and internationally by Penguin Random House Publisher Services.

Berrett-Koehler and the BK logo are registered trademarks of Berrett-Koehler Publishers, Inc.

Printed in the United States of America

Berrett-Koehler books are printed on long-lasting acid-free paper. When it is available, we choose paper that has been manufactured by environmentally responsible processes. These may include using trees grown in sustainable forests, incorporating recycled paper, minimizing chlorine in bleaching, or recycling the energy produced at the paper mill.

Library of Congress Cataloging-in-Publication Data

Names: Stout, Lynn A., 1957- | Gramitto, Sergio. | Belinfanti, Tamara.
   Title: Citizen capitalism : how a universal fund can provide influence and
      income to all / Lynn Stout, Sergio Gramitto, Tamara Belinfanti.
   Description: Oakland, CA : Berrett-Koehler Publishers, Inc., [2019] |
      Includes bibliographical references and index.
   Identifiers: LCCN 2018043625 | ISBN 9781523095650 (print paperpack)
   Subjects: LCSH: Guaranteed annual income. | Capitalism. | Free enterprise. |
      Citizenship.
   Classification: LCC HC79.I5 .S787 2019 | DDC 362.5/82--dc23
   LC record available at https://lccn.loc.gov/2018043625

First Edition

23 22 21 20 19 18   10 9 8 7 6 5 4 3 2 1

Interior design and production: Dovetail Publishing Services
Cover design: M.80 Design, Wes Youssi
Cover illustration: Shutterstock.com

To all our children

Contents

In Memoriam

Lynn Stout

Preface

WE ARE NOT UNTETHERED IDEALISTS. With a combined experience of more than sixty years in corporate governance as lawyers and scholars, we understand that business corporations provide enormous value in many forms, including salaries, employee benefits, health care, useful innovations, tax revenues, and philanthropic donations. Yet at the same time, we know that corporate behavior can have negative repercussions, such as environmental pollution, unfair labor practices, and gender pay gaps, to name a few.

These results are inextricably linked to the underlying nature of today's corporate governance system, which has been dominated by a myopic focus on short-term financial results at the expense of long-term performance. This in turn results in a vicious cycle, which includes reducing expenditures on research and development; decisions that harm employees, customers, and communities; and actions that on the face of it seem reckless and socially irresponsible. In short, given the historical norm of shareholder value and the nature in which shares are often voted, the corporate sector's potential for addressing broader economic, social, and political problems has not been optimized.

A few years ago we began to specifically focus on a precise question: Is there a way to address the flaws in our corporate governance system in a manner that helps address a number of these economic, social, and environmental threats? It is this question that gave rise to this book, and we believe the answer is "yes."

This book offers a simple plan for harnessing the power of corporations to save ourselves and our future. It is a plan that is structured around free enterprise, it requires no government funding, it involves no forced redistribution of wealth, and it is completely voluntary and will not force anyone to do anything they object to. Unlike many other proposals, our plan does not sacrifice one value to support another. We call our project Citizen Capitalism.

At the heart of it lies the creation of a Universal Fund, which is based on a mutual fund model, but with several key exceptions, all of which are designed to broaden access and opportunity for everyday citizens to participate in capital markets. In addition, our Universal Fund model is designed to shift critical leverage points in our economic system and unlock the enormous potential of corporations to be a positive force for good.

We have written this book for anyone interested in having a role in building a better future. In it, we offer up to you and to the world a practical blueprint for the creation of the Universal Fund. We describe a very direct way to participate in making the Universal Fund a reality at the end of this book, and at CitCap.org you can receive information on events and join discussions.[1]

As you read through this book and learn more about this transformative plan, and as you come to share our appreciation of its deeply positive potential impact, we invite you to take stock of your skills, your talents, your experience—and then ask yourself what you can do to participate in Citizen Capitalism.

Introduction

What If?

CHANGE BEGINS WITH IMAGINING something better. In this book, we offer a proposal for reengineering the relationship between citizens and corporations in a manner that would address a wide range of social problems, including but not limited to rising inequality; racial tensions; increasing poverty, unemployment, and income insecurity; low levels of innovation and investment; corporate mistreatment of customers, employees, and communities; climate change and environmental destruction; and dysfunctions in the political system.

In the process of helping address a striking number of economic, social, and environmental threats, our plan would promote civic engagement, reduce popular discontent, and help heal our politically divided society.

Our strategy requires no new government funding, demands no new taxes, and does not force anyone to do anything that they object to.

In these pages we describe a pragmatic plan for building a better society and a brighter future for all, through a strategy that benefits almost everyone and harms no one. Our approach is based on this insight: governments are not the only powerful institutions that can solve our collective social and economic problems. Another type of force can be brought to bear. This other force rivals nation-states in its weight, influence, and reach. It is more responsive, more agile, and more efficient than any government could hope to be. It controls enormous resources that can be quickly put to work solving our most critical and intractable problems, including poverty, disease, and climate change. This great force is our business corporations.

Business corporations today control tens of trillions of dollars in assets, generate tens of trillions of dollars of goods and services, and affect hundreds of millions of customers, employees, and shareholders. They touch every area of our lives. They benefit all of us enormously by providing not only innovative products and services but also employment opportunities, investment returns, and tax revenues. They provide critical benefits to us and to future generations by developing the kinds of new technologies that are essential to sustained economic growth:[1] railroads and manufacturing plants in the 1800s; cars, electricity, and computers in the 1900s; self-driving cars and space vehicles today. Yet corporations can also inflict great harms: environmental damage, consumer frauds, employee deaths and injuries, political corruption.

Most of us recognize that corporations have an enormous impact on our society but think of them as beyond our influence. We tend to view corporations as an irresistible force that helps or harms, but remains outside average citizens' control. Supreme Court justice Louis Brandeis once famously described the corporation as a "Frankenstein's monster."[2] As experts in corporate governance, we know this does not have to be true. It is possible to tame corporations so they better serve humanity. In fact, engaging the power of business corporations may be essential to solving our most pressing economic and social problems.

Indeed, not engaging the power of corporations is a lost opportunity. In 2013, for example, Royal Dutch Shell cut back on its already-small investment in biofuel research on the grounds the technology could not be commercially viable until 2020 or later.[3] As we write, 2018 has already arrived. Take a moment to imagine where we might be today if three decades ago, when one of the world's largest fossil fuel companies became aware of the risks of climate change, the industry had chosen to focus its efforts on addressing the problem. If companies like Exxon, BP, Shell, and Chevron had put their billions of dollars of profits into investigating and developing cleaner energy alternatives, we might already have, or be on the cusp of having abundant and affordable clean energy.

Our plan provides a new way of addressing the fatal flaws in today's corporate governance system that keep corporations from reaching their full potential to serve humanity. And it would do this in a fashion that ameliorates aspects of social equality.

A Dividing Nation

By any number of measures, the gap between the most and the least well-off Americans is alarmingly large, and growing. The top 1 percent of wealth holders now control nearly 40 percent of the nation's wealth.[4] The income reaped by top earners is growing while the wages of the middle class stagnate.[5] Socioeconomic mobility is declining; between 1981 and 2008, the probability of an American moving significantly higher or lower in the earnings distribution during their working career declined significantly.[6] We are even seeing growing differences in life expectancy. A study in the *Journal of the American Medical Association* found that from 2001 to 2014, the life expectancy of those in the top 5 percent of pretax income rose by nearly three years, while the life expectancy of those in the bottom 5 percent increased less than three months. The life expectancy of the richest 1 percent of American men is now fifteen years more than that of the poorest 1 percent (ten years more for the top 1 percent of women).[7]

There is no sign the trend will stop. To the contrary, thought leaders on both the Right and Left are concerned that the rich are becoming richer in part because they can use their wealth to buy political influence that allows them to acquire even more wealth. Hedge fund managers lobby politicians for loopholes in the tax code;[8] giant corporations squash competitors while regulators stand by. Wealth and income inequality feeds on itself, widening the gap between citizens.

Our plan would fight this trend by reducing inequality in at least two ways. First, it will generate greater equality in influence over corporations. Second, it will supplement income. Every citizen would benefit more from the corporate sector, and the corporate sector would benefit from the engagement of all citizens.

The same is true for many other critical challenges society faces, including infrastructure decay, poverty, chronic and acute disease, and the problem of caring for an aging population. Too many corporations neglect such issues to focus instead on the short-term goal of raising share price—no matter the cost to employees, consumers, taxpayers, or even the integrity of our political system.

The Solution: Citizen Capitalism

We have written this book to offer a realistic way to help our corporations do better at helping all, and to potentially heal the growing divisions in our society. We do not propose a radical restructuring of society or offer some vision of a future utopia. Rather, we offer a plan that is relatively simple and can be easily implemented in the near future. Our strategy relies on the power of private ordering—the voluntary actions of private individuals coming together of their own free will to solve collective problems. Our plan's effects may be modest at first, but they are structured to grow over time. Its basic elements are few and straightforward.

1. We envision the private creation of a Universal Fund (Fund) that would be somewhat similar to a typical mutual fund. Each US citizen age eighteen years or older would be eligible to receive a share in the Universal Fund (citizen-share) and so become a citizen-shareholder.

2. The Universal Fund would assemble a portfolio of stocks in different corporations. These would be acquired primarily from donations from corporations and individuals, especially the ultrawealthy.

3. On a regular basis, the Universal Fund would pass on the income received from the stocks in its portfolio (primarily dividends and cash from share repurchases) directly to its citizen-shareholders in equal proportion.

4. Citizen-shareholders would not be allowed to buy, sell, or bequeath their citizen-shares. They would hold their citizen-shares for life, and after death their interest in their citizen-shares would revert to the Fund. Thus, as donations continue to be made, the Fund will continue to grow.

5. Just as citizen-shareholders cannot trade their shares, the Universal Fund cannot trade the stocks in its portfolio but must hold them indefinitely. This means neither the Fund nor its citizen-shareholders have an interest in manipulating short-term share prices.

6. The Universal Fund would give its citizen-shareholders a political right to vote the shares of each company's

stock held in its portfolio. To make voting convenient and informed, the Universal Fund would allow citizen-shareholders the opportunity to use Fund-approved "proxy advisor services" that would be paid for by the Fund. While most people have probably never heard of proxy advisory firms, they play an important role in corporate elections today. For a fee, proxy advisors issue voting guidance to institutional shareholders on how to vote the stocks in their portfolio and will even do the job of actually casting the votes.

The remaining chapters of this book explain the features of Citizen Capitalism in greater detail. They also explore the wide range of potential social and economic benefits it offers and address possible questions and challenges. First, though, we would like to highlight two key reasons why Citizen Capitalism is quite different from most other reform proposals that have been offered on both the Right and the Left—and, we believe, why it is far more likely to enjoy broad support, to be implemented, and to actually work. The first reason is that Citizen Capitalism harnesses the vast and relatively untapped power of the corporate sector to address public problems. The second is that it does this without any new taxes or government funding.

Harnessing Corporate Power to Solve Social and Economic Problems

Many people believe that corporations have one and only one purpose: to make their shareholders (maybe even just a subset of shareholders) as wealthy as possible. As we explain in later chapters, this is both an erroneous and impoverished view of what corporations can and should do.[9] It's perfectly possible to harness the power of the *$40 trillion* (that's trillion, with a T) in assets that business corporations control today and use that power not only to reap sustainable profits but to solve society's biggest problems.[10]

Citizen Capitalism can liberate corporations from the tyranny of "shareholder value" and free them to better serve our diverse, long-term human interests. The key to understanding how this dream can become a reality lies in understanding the current patterns in how shares of business corporations are owned, traded, and voted. First, both stock ownership and the economic benefits it confers are concentrated in the hands of older, whiter, and wealthier Americans. This is cause enough for concern in an era of rising economic inequality and insecurity. But shareholder power over our largest corporations—power over the economic heart of our nation and over our collective future—has been concentrated even further and now rests in the hands of a narrow group of special interests that often does not have much stake in the fates of the companies whose shares they control, but does have great ability to use that power to enrich themselves. It is these narrow interests that relentlessly pressure corporations to "maximize shareholder value"—an abstract goal that almost always translates into the mindless, short-term pursuit of a higher stock price. The outcome has been a system that enriches a very few while often harming average shareholders and especially average citizens.

Most Americans, whether they own stocks or not, care about more than just a company's current stock price. They also care about customer service, about employment security, about preserving a strong middle class, about enjoying a secure retirement, about the integrity of our political system, about the quality of their environment, about the health of their planet, and about our children and grandchildren. Yet even though more than half of American households still invest in the stock market either directly or through pension and mutual funds, their voices—and the voices of those who do not own shares—are rarely heard in the boardroom. Citizen Capitalism can change this by creating and empowering a new class of long-term, diverse shareholders who can change the direction of Corporate America, making corporations more citizens' servants—and less citizens' masters.

Private Ordering, Not Government or Market Forces

A second important and novel element of our plan is that, as mentioned, it relies entirely on the voluntary actions of private individuals coming together of their own free will. Academics call this "private ordering," and it has been used throughout history to create a wide range of powerful institutions and organizations. Private ordering differs from a simple market-based exchange. It is a specific type of voluntary association that typically involves the development of rules and norms by private entities without necessarily requiring state involvement. Private ordering has been used throughout history, from the Middle Ages to our current digital age, to create powerful institutions and organizations that serve collective interests. Organizations as diverse as Princeton University, the New York Stock Exchange, and the Red Cross are all models of private ordering.

Citizen Capitalism avoids the trap of trying to address society's current challenges exclusively through either government or free markets. Through a new privately ordered organization—the Universal Fund—we can channel the tremendous power of our corporate sector and use its immense resources more wisely. And we can do this without either waiting for government funding or allowing ourselves to be held hostage to uncontrolled market forces. We need not choose between laissez-faire and central planning. Citizen Capitalism offers an entirely different alternative path toward a better future—a path that bridges the tired and divisive debate between those labeled "liberal" and "conservative." Through a strategy that benefits everyone and coerces no one, it promises to bring us closer together and to heal our divided nation.

An Outline of This Book

Chapters 1 and 2 sketch the state of the corporate sector today. We show how the current corporate governance system concentrates control over society's corporate sector in the hands of a small, nonrepresentative group of interests, many of whom don't even own the shares whose votes they control, and most of whom drive companies to focus on short-term increases in share price or accounting profits without regard to resulting harms to employees, customers, the environment, or other shareholders.

Chapter 3 outlines the framework for the Universal Fund. It also explains why the Fund, and the proxy advisors we envision, would do a much better job of authentically serving the interests of citizen-shareholders than the mutual funds or proxy services we see today.

Chapter 4 explores why we believe a Universal Fund built on private ordering is a feasible venture—the private money is there, as is a robust philanthropic culture.

Chapter 5 discusses how Citizen Capitalism can increase broader participation in corporate governance. By creating a powerful new class of long-term, diverse citizen-shareholders, and by giving them an informed collective voice, Citizen Capitalism can make corporations more sensitive to the interests of average citizens—and by doing so, perhaps make many politicians more sensitive to those interests as well. A somewhat unique benefit of our plan is that it promotes equality in influence among Americans, especially influence over corporations. By bringing more real democracy to our corporate sector,

Citizen Capitalism can shift the direction of the corporate sector in a number of desirable ways. Unlike the interest groups that control so many corporations today, the Universal Fund provides a vehicle for citizen-shareholders to focus on long-term results and support the type of corporate research and investment that ultimately produces important innovations, bigger profits, investment returns, and greater economic growth. Citizen-shareholders might also have more reason to care about the impacts corporations have on the environment, our political system, and on employees, customers, and taxpayers—that is, on citizen-shareholders themselves. By making their voices heard in the boardroom, and by challenging the flawed and erroneous mantra of "shareholder value," Citizen Capitalism could channel the tremendous power and resources of the corporate sector to build a better and more prosperous future for everyone.

Chapters 6, 7, and 8 discuss some of the benefits of Citizen Capitalism outside of the corporate governance sphere and in relation to broader societal problems. Chapter 6 shows how Citizen Capitalism simultaneously harnesses the power of capitalism while inculcating other values such as openness and transparency; hope for and investment in the future; and responsibility, including responsibility to the generations that will follow us. Chapter 7 begins by discussing how Citizen Capitalism is not only consistent with but actively reinforces widely embraced values historically associated with American culture and the "American Dream." These values include equal opportunity, personal liberty, and civic engagement. In today's insecure, divided, and even angry society, many of these values seem at risk. Citizen Capitalism can help restore them to their rightful place. Chapter 8 discusses how Citizen Capitalism could help promote economic equality and equal opportunity. A Universal Fund would allow all US citizens—including young people and less wealthy people—to reap a share of the financial benefits generated by the corporations that are the engines of the economy.

Chapter 9 examines how the Universal Fund and the broader Citizen Capitalism project compare to Universal Basic Income (UBI) proposals, citizens' dividend proposals, and redistribution proposals in general. We show how the Universal Fund achieves many of the same goals as UBI proposals, but with two distinct advantages—first, our plan does not rely on government funding, and second, our plan does not rely on government-directed redistributions of wealth.

Chapter 10 addresses the critical question: Why not Citizen Capitalism? We argue that the primary obstacles to creating a Universal Fund are, in fact, purely psychological—in particular, the beliefs that people are always narrowly selfish, that only government or free markets can solve problems, and that anything that hasn't been done in the past cannot be done in the future. If we can overcome these erroneous habits of thought, Citizen Capitalism offers a pragmatic path toward making the world a better place and the United States a stronger nation.

We conclude with the question "What Next?" because Citizen Capitalism *can* happen; it is not a matter of "if," it is a matter of "how."

Most of us understand the importance of democratic processes in ensuring that governments serve their citizens. We can reap similar benefits by promoting more real democracy in corporations. By making the corporate sector more democratic, Citizen Capitalism makes it better: more fair, more productive, more representative of citizens' authentic interests, and more resilient, sustainable, and profitable. We need more than a democratic political system. If we want to have a fair and open society and to solve a number of" collective problems, we need Citizen Capitalism.

This book shows how to build it. It should interest anyone who studies or thinks about how to create a sustainable future, as well as those interested in economic and social policy. And it should offer hope to anyone who cares about the economy, the political system, or our descendants. For those interested, in the conclusion we offer suggestions for how we each can make Citizen Capitalism a reality.[11]

Chapter 1

Lost Opportunity

How do societies decide who gets what and what gets done? Most people pondering this question think of two controlling forces: free markets and government. Together they seem to rule our lives, determining how we live (For example, have I saved enough to buy a house? Are the neighborhood schools good here?); what we do (Can I afford a vacation? What's the speed limit here?), and what we consume (Can I pay for a new smartphone? Do I need a prescription to buy that drug?). In general, liberals tend to favor relying on government to solve social problems, while conservatives often prefer relying on the market. But whatever our political leanings, most of us think of governments and markets as the two options for solving problems and allocating resources.

Beyond Governments and Markets

There's a third force, however, that also governs us: private ordering. Academics use private ordering to describe institutions and organizations that exercise control over people's lives yet are created through the voluntary actions of private individuals coming together of their own free will. Just as governments and markets have existed for thousands of years, so too have powerful private organizations. Many of our greatest universities are private organizations, including Princeton, Yale, Harvard,

Stanford, Cambridge, and Oxford. The Sierra Club (three million members),[1] the AARP (thirty-eight million members),[2] National Public Radio (thirty-five million weekly listeners),[3] the New York Stock Exchange, and the Smithsonian Institution (approximately thirty million annual visitors)[4] are all private organizations. So, too, are the residential co-ops and condominium associations in which millions of Americans live today.[5]

What makes privately ordered organizations different from markets and governments? First, unlike an open marketplace, where the only "law" is that you must be willing and able to pay for something, privately ordered organizations impose and enforce detailed rules of behavior on the people inside them. Students must follow the honor code or be sanctioned. Employees must be present during work hours unless excused. Companies must meet certain qualifications or the NYSE will refuse to list them. Moreover, private organizations often make decisions and act through a complex process that involves many different individuals and groups, and they may use governance techniques like voting, delegation of authority, higher-level review, and checks and balances that resemble those we see in political systems. As a result, very large private organizations look a lot like governments and can even be described as quasi-governments.

But there's a key difference between privately ordered organizations and the state: unlike government regulations, the regulations of private organizations can be avoided simply by choosing not to deal with the organization. You can choose to ride with Lyft, with Uber, or not at all. You can choose not to apply to a particular university. You can choose not to list a company on the NYSE. But you can't choose not to pay taxes—at least, not without going to jail or paying a large fine. A private organization's internal rules don't apply to anyone who doesn't want to deal with the organization. If, however, you want to do business/deal with such an organization, you must follow the rules, and the punishment for violations is typically exclusion from the benefits provided by the organization—whether it be a club, a university, or a business corporation.

Enter the Business Corporation

The most powerful of our private institutions—the Leviathans swimming in our economic seas—are business corporations. To get a sense of just how powerful and pervasive this third force truly is, it's worth comparing corporate power and influence with that of the federal government. In 2016, the federal government took in $3.3 trillion in revenues.[6] The Global 500—the world's biggest five hundred companies by revenue according to *Fortune* magazine's ranking—brought in nearly ten times as much, $27 trillion.[7] The federal government has 2.25 million civilian employees.[8] Walmart alone has more—2.3 million.[9]

Like other privately ordered organizations, business corporations are formed through the voluntary actions of free individuals. Yet collectively, in many ways they dictate the structure and content of our lives. Modern life makes it nearly impossible to escape dealing with business corporations. While you might be able to escape dealing with private clubs, universities, or religious groups, imagine how difficult your life would be if you tried to avoid interacting with corporations. They affect what we can and cannot do, what we do or do not have, how we spend our days, and even—in the case of the health insurance industry—how we choose our doctors and make decisions that could affect our health.

If you think of your typical day, perhaps you rise in the morning and learn what's happened in the world from Facebook, Twitter, Fox News, CNN, or the *New York Times*. You drink coffee from Starbucks or tea from Lipton. You take Lyft to work or drive a Toyota. At some point before reaching work you check your emails and texts (hopefully not while driving) on your Samsung or Apple smartphone, over a network powered by Verizon, AT&T, or T-Mobile. Once at work, your workplace itself may be a corporation—UPS, Walmart, IBM, or Citibank. In the evening you get groceries from Whole Foods or Kroger, or a burger from Sonic, Shake Shack, or McDonald's. That night you watch Netflix or Hulu, or search YouTube, or do a little online shopping with Amazon. Maybe you check how your IRA is doing (if you are lucky enough to have one) at Charles Schwab or Fidelity. A life without interfacing with corporations would mean you would have no cell phone, no means to get around outside the city center, no retirement investment fund, and very possibly no shelter or food beyond what you could build, grow, or scavenge yourself. (And even the few individuals who manage to live "off the grid" are affected when corporations dirty the air, pollute the waters, or change the climate.)

Where Corporations Go Right

Luckily, while corporations pervade our lives, they also provide us with a lot of very useful inventions and social contributions. In the nineteenth century, corporations built the railroads, steel mills, and factories that powered the Industrial Revolution and tremendously improved most people's standard of living. In the early twentieth century, General Electric and Consolidated Edison built the electrical grid, while Otis Elevator Company developed and produced the electric elevators that made high-rise buildings and modern cities possible. In the late twentieth century, IBM created personal computers, and Google developed the search engines that allowed easy access to information on the internet. Today, Tesla and Alphabet are working on self-driving cars, while Pfizer and AstraZeneca seek cures for cancer.

In the process of creating and producing critical new technologies, corporations give us a cornucopia of other benefits: salaries and jobs training for workers, dividends and interest payments for investors, quality goods and services for consumers, tax payments for governments, infrastructure and philanthropic donations for communities. Consider the example of Corning Incorporated, a Fortune 500 company headquartered in New York State's Southern Tier region, between the authors' hometowns of Ithaca and Brooklyn. Corning has an enviable record of innovation, having developed the glass used in Thomas Edison's light bulbs, the fiber optic cables that underlie the modern telecommunications system, and the tough "gorilla glass" that covers most smartphones today. These inventions are wonderful social contributions.

But Corning does much more. It employs more than forty thousand people.[10] In 2016, it paid its shareholders $645 million in dividends, while authorizing more than $4 billion to repurchase some of its shares from investors.[11] Moreover, the Corning Incorporated Foundation makes millions of dollars of grants to local and regional educational, cultural, volunteer, and human services programs.[12]

Where Corporations Go Wrong

Corning might have a less impressive record, however, when it comes to contributing its share to the public treasury. Reportedly, by stashing more than $10 billion in offshore tax havens, it was able to pay no federal income taxes at all between 2008 and 2012.[13] And when Corning doesn't pay taxes, the rest of us have to pay more.

As Corning's tax strategy demonstrates, while corporations provide us with a number of essential benefits, they could do better. There are many critical human problems our corporations have failed to solve—in some cases, failed to even seriously address. These include the scourges of poverty, disease, pollution, and climate change.

Let us consider the case of climate change. Climate change is already bringing us droughts, floods, heat waves, shrinking glaciers, rising sea levels, invasive pests, dying coral reefs, infectious diseases, and extreme weather events that threaten our infrastructure, agriculture, fisheries, and many industries—as well as our health and our ecosystem. Its costs have been estimated at more than $240 billion over the past ten years in the United States alone and can only be expected to rise in the future.[14] Of course, most of us have contributed our share of carbon to the atmosphere. But we have few attractive alternatives; fossil fuels remain our cheapest and most readily available source of energy. The fossil fuel industry has played a major role in ensuring they remain so, devoting enormous resources to lobbying against a carbon tax, funding scientists who question climate change, and developing environmentally destructive, energy-intensive fuel extraction technologies like fracking.[15]

The same is true for many other difficult problems we face today, including poverty, crumbling infrastructure, chronic and acute disease, and our nation's need to protect and preserve an accurate, informed, effective, and untainted mass media. Too many companies neglect such issues to focus instead on goals like cutting costs or raising revenues—no matter the cost to employees, consumers, taxpayers, or the integrity of our political system.

Corporations contain both *yin* and *yang*. In the process of producing desirable things, corporations can produce less desirable things as well. Uber makes local travel cheaper, but its business model is destroying a taxi industry that arguably provided more secure jobs for drivers. Facebook and Twitter have allowed us to connect and communicate online with many more people, but they may be making our relationships shallower and promoting narcissism and loneliness.[16] The fossil fuel industry's fracking technologies have reduced energy costs while threatening our water supply and contributing to climate change. Meanwhile, the finance and tech industries have contributed to growing economic inequality and the rise of an ultrawealthy elite with outsized wealth, power, and influence, while doing disproportionately less to address concerns at the bottom of the pyramid. As we discuss below, the mistaken mantra of shareholder value is often used as the main justification for why corporations do not extend their capacities to addressing social concerns.

The Mistaken Mantra of Shareholder Value

One obstacle to better corporations is the common—but erroneous—belief that corporations must maximize "shareholder value." In her 2012 book, *The Shareholder Value Myth: How Putting Shareholders First Harms Companies, Investors, and the Public*,[17] author Lynn Stout explains at length why this is false. Interested readers can learn more there, but the bottom line is easily summarized.

The idea that corporations should maximize shareholder value draws most of its power from the arguments of late twentieth-century "Chicago School" economists like Milton Friedman. In reality, US corporate law is quite flexible about what goals corporations must pursue. Corporate law is mostly state law, and state codes explicitly allow corporations to be formed "for any lawful purpose." Virtually all corporate charters describe the company's purpose in similar language (the authors have never seen a charter listing a company's purpose as "maximizing shareholder value"). Meanwhile, judges deciding corporate law cases religiously apply a doctrine called the business judgment rule to protect disinterested directors from liability for failing to maximize profits or stock price. Occasionally, a judge trained during the height of the Chicago School's influence—judges are as vulnerable to culture as anyone else—may vaguely suggest in an opinion that corporate directors have an amorphous, and never actually enforced, duty to maximize profits. Such musings, however, are mere "dicta" that other judges are free to ignore. And plenty of contrary dicta can be found. Consider US Supreme Court justice Samuel Alito's recent statement in *Burwell v. Hobby Lobby Stores* that "modern corporate law does not require for-profit corporations to pursue profit at the expense of everything else, and many do not do so."[18]

Second, trying to "maximize shareholder value" is not only *not* a legal requirement, it is often a bad business idea, especially in the long run. Long-term investors don't care much about today's stock price; they care about the company's future performance. Unfortunately, without a crystal ball, it is impossible to quantify future performance in a fashion everyone can agree with. This means that attempts to increase shareholder value in a way that can be measured today inevitably translate into attempts to raise short-term metrics like stock price or current earnings—metrics that can be gamed by selling off assets, taking on debt, or cutting "expenses" such as payroll or research and development. As Larry Fink, famed CEO of BlackRock mutual funds, publicly complained in his 2016 annual letter to CEOs, such a focus on short-term results harms long-term shareholders, who would prefer companies devote their attention to developing new products and markets.[19]

Meanwhile, chasing shareholder value not only hurts long-term corporate results, it also harms shareholders' broader interests as diversified investors, employees, consumers, taxpayers, and organisms that must live in the environment.

When company after company relentlessly lays off employees to boost the bottom line, overall unemployment rises, consumer demand falls, and eventually corporate profits suffer. Similarly, when fossil fuel companies seek profits from fracking instead of developing cleaner energy technologies, what we gain as investors is more than wiped out by what we lose from dealing with hurricanes, heat waves, tainted water supplies, droughts, floods, new tropical diseases, or climate change–driven political instability.

Nor are we the only ones who lose. For example, climate change not only imposes enormous costs on the current generation; it also harms future generations, other species, and the planet.

Another fatal flaw in the "shareholder value" mantra is that it ignores the reality that most people would prefer their companies not make profits by breaking the law, abusing employees, defrauding consumers, polluting the environment, corrupting the political system, or impoverishing future generations. Science supports this view; hundreds of experiments have demonstrated that the vast majority of human beings are inclined toward what scientists call "prosocial" behavior (and you wouldn't want your son or daughter to marry someone who wasn't).[20] Yes, we want our companies to be profitable most of the time and to provide decent investment returns. But we don't want them to "maximize" those returns at the expense of our values. As Canadian professor and activist Joel Bakan has warned in the award-winning book and documentary *The Corporation*, when a corporation is run to maximize profits without regard to ethics, the law, or human welfare, the result is a "psychopathic" creature.[21] Most of us don't want to act like, benefit from, or be vulnerable to psychopaths—especially psychopaths that are incredibly powerful and touch our lives every day.

Ironically, even in the face of shareholder value norms, examples of corporations applying their know-how and expertise to address poverty and other social concerns while still generating financial value prove that corporate social engineering does not have to be a zero-sum game. The following case studies offer a case in point.

Case Study 1: Hindustan Unilever Limited

Unilever is a global company with over four hundred brands, including well-known products like Dove soap, Lipton tea, and Magnum ice cream bars.[22] The company estimates that "seven out of ten households around the world contain at least one Unilever product."[23] However, several years ago the company recognized that there were a number of rural villages in India that had no access to its products. At the same time, an employee at Unilever recognized that many of these rural villages had high rates of unemployment and in addition, the segment of the population that was most likely to be unemployed was women. From this insight, Unilever set out to develop a strategy that would bridge the corporation's interest in successfully reaching what were thought to be inaccessible rural markets while addressing the problem of rural unemployment. Unilever developed Project Shakti, an initiative that employs women in rural villages to distribute Unilever's products. Or as the company describes it, "Project Shakti is an initiative to financially empower rural women and create livelihood opportunities for them. It provides a regular income stream for the Shakti entrepreneurs and their families."[24] The word "Shakti" means strength and empowerment, and it is also the name of a Hindu goddess. Through Project Shakti, Unilever trains women entrepreneurs ("Shakti Ammas") in the basics of distribution management and the company's product line, providing them with a regular income stream, and in return Unilever is able to develop its distribution channels. Project Shakti currently employs approximately eighty thousand Shakti Ammas in India and is an exemplar of corporations strategically using their expertise to drive social change.[25] As such, Unilever has created variations on its Shakti model in Bangladesh, Egypt, Sri Lanka, and Vietnam.

Case Study 2: Grameen Danone

Danone is a large global corporation and leader in the food industry, whose brands include Oikos yogurt, Volvic water, and its Danone yogurt line.[26] Danone's products are available in more than 120 countries, it employs over one hundred thousand people spread across 60 countries, and its annual sales totaled approximately $28.6 billion in 2017.[27] One of the countries in which Danone has a presence is Bangladesh. Bangladesh has a high rate of malnutrition, with approximately 30 percent of all Bangladeshis and 56 percent of all Bangladeshi children under the age of five suffering from moderate to severe malnutrition.[28] In 2006, Danone embarked on a project in Bangladesh (Grameen Danone—a joint venture between Danone and the Bangladeshi government) to develop an enriched yogurt with essential nutrients that could be delivered at a price point well below Danone's traditional model.[29] To succeed, Danone needed to develop a yogurt that contained enough key nutrients, like vitamin A, iron, and zinc, in one 60–80 mg cup, to deliver 30 percent of a child's daily nutritional needs. This was unlike anything the company had previously undertaken, but through knowledge sharing with an NGO, it learned of a less reactive iron that could be used in the product. The product was a success in achieving its goals. In turn, Danone has taken the know-how it developed in creating the enriched yogurt product for the Bangladeshi market and has used this less reactive iron in products sold in developed markets, including the United States.

The Opportunity

Unilever and Danone are not alone in their efforts to unite corporate strength and strategy with sustainability and social value. Examples of corporations leveraging their know-how for social good are not as rare as one might think.[30] Other examples include Vodafone's use of its mobile technology know-how to provide access to banking in Kenya, and Microsoft's "Unlimited Potential Group," which focuses on bringing affordable technology to low-income market segments.

So, if corporations are not required by law to maximize short-term financial returns, and if trying to do so often harms long-term, diversified, nonpsychopathic investors, why don't corporate managers recognize this and do better? As we shall see, the answer lies in who or what truly controls our corporations. Average Americans who own shares directly do not vote their shares ("vote their shares" is a term of art meaning that, as owners of stock in a corporation, they have the right to vote in a number of corporate matters). Those who own shares indirectly oftentimes leave their right to vote in the hands of their pension fund or mutual fund manager, who in turn is supposed to represent their interests. However, the interests of fund managers may oftentimes differ from the interests of the individual who has long-term investment goals. Mutual fund managers are typically judged and compensated based on how their portfolio has performed over a relatively short time frame (for example, the last few quarters or at the most the last few years) and traditionally have had very little incentive to think about human welfare and other social concerns when evaluating the companies in their portfolio. The business model of other institutional shareholders, such as hedge funds, also makes it unlikely to expect that such investors would be incentivized to push corporations toward being a more positive force for good.

Yet the fact remains that business corporations have immense power to do good and not so good things. The better question is whether we can shift our corporate sector even further in the direction of doing good and further away from doing bad. Can we ensure that the benefits flowing from the business corporations that are the engines of the economy are shared more broadly? Can we better harness the power of the $40,000,000,000,000 in assets business corporations control today[31] and focus them on solving society's biggest problems?

The creation of the Universal Fund we envision would act as a recalibrating force in the market and do just that. It would create a new type of institutional investor that truly holds for the long term while providing citizens with influence over the corporate sector. The Universal Fund would be an aggregator of the voice of all citizen-shareholders, representing their long-term interests and expectations in corporate governance. Citizen Capitalism elevates, coordinates, and aggregates the collective interests of average citizens. Put differently, the Universal Fund provides a vehicle for a broader swath of American society to have voice in the corporate sector. As we shall see in the next chapter, understanding the role and motivations of key players in corporate governance is key to understanding the points of leverage in the system.

Chapter 2

Short-Termism and Corporate Governance

GENERALLY SPEAKING, THE PHRASE "corporate governance" describes the processes corporations use to make decisions—to pay dividends, raise employee salaries, introduce new products, hire or fire the CEO, and almost every other matter. The subject can be mind-numbingly boring and technical. Most people would rather have a root canal than try to understand even its basic elements. Perhaps this is why narrow special interests have been able to quietly capture control over the immense public companies that are the beating heart of our economy and in many circumstances use that control to serve themselves.

If you want to understand what makes corporations tick— if you want to understand what's gone wrong with our system, how it's harming our people and our nation, and how we can fix it—you need to take a deep breath and plunge in. We will try to make the lesson as painless as possible. We can promise you that when we are done, you will be disturbed to learn that corporations don't work the way most people think they do—and the reality of modern corporate governance might be hazardous to America's health.

It's important to note that the governance system we are about to describe does not apply to all incorporated entities, many of which are small businesses that consist of nothing more than an email address and single shareholder who is also the business's only employee. The corporations we are interested in are the big ones, especially the "public" companies whose shares can be purchased by average investors—the GEs, the Microsofts, the Amazons. Public companies are few in number—fewer than four thousand in the United States, compared to the millions of small "private" corporations that file corporate tax returns[1]— but they dominate our economy and our lives. And the forces that determine what they do and how they do it merit attention.

We will begin by introducing the different groups that play the most important roles in the decision-making process of big corporations. For our purposes, the most important players in corporate governance are: (1) the corporate entity itself, (2) boards of directors, (3) shareholders, (4) mutual and pension fund portfolio managers, (5) the behind-the-scenes but enormously important organizations known as "proxy advisors," and, finally (6) hedge funds. Alert readers may have noticed we have not listed corporate executives, not even the CEO. We'll explain why soon. And we will introduce you to two significant institutions that you've likely never heard of: Institutional Shareholder Services (ISS) and Glass Lewis.

Player 1: The Corporation Itself

Let us begin with the corporate entity. Nonexperts often say corporations "belong" to their shareholders. This is a dangerous mistake—just because you own stock in Tesla doesn't mean you can stroll into the factory and help yourself to a Model S. In the eyes of the law, a corporation is an independent "legal person" with its own rights, including the rights to own property and to enter into contracts. This is why it's misleading to say shareholders have "limited liability" for corporate debts. As a general rule, *no human* has liability for a corporation's debts—only the corporate entity itself does. Also, the fact that corporations are legal persons does not mean they enjoy the same rights natural persons enjoy. For example, no court has given corporations a right to vote in presidential elections.

Shareholders and the corporations in which they own stock are not the same thing. This is a useful and important distinction, because shareholders are mortal and corporations are not. In fact, state corporate codes grant corporations "perpetual" existence as one of their default characteristics. As "perpetual entities," corporations have the ability to make investments and pursue projects that will take decades, even generations, to complete. That may be why they were invented. In the Middle Ages, corporate entities were used to build cathedrals and universities. In the eighteenth and nineteenth centuries they built canals and railroads. In the twentieth, they developed the electrical grid, air travel, and the internet. Today they're working on self-driving cars and space travel.

Player 2: The Board of Directors

Corporations are legal persons, but they are not natural persons: they don't have brains, or arms and legs. So, how do they decide and act? The answer is: through ever-shifting pools of human beings, especially their boards of directors. Corporate law gives the board the ultimate authority to control what the corporation does, provided the board follows prescribed decision-making procedures. For example, meetings must be held in person or by conference call, a quorum must be present, majority vote decides, and so forth.

Boards of directors are peculiar institutions. Often their members have little or no connection with the company beyond their board position. Directors typically spend only part of their time being directors and are paid relatively little compared to what the company's executives are paid. Yet directors have nearly unfettered discretion to make decisions on the company's behalf. Their decisions are constrained by their fiduciary duties—the duty of care and the duty of loyalty. It is their "fiduciary duty of loyalty" that severely restricts their ability to take any money out of the company beyond their relatively modest director fees.

If directors' positions are part-time and not especially well paid (relatively speaking), how can we expect boards to manage the day-to-day operations of large corporations? The answer is: we don't. Boards are free to, and usually do, delegate much corporate decision-making and responsibility for taking action to the executive team they select, especially the chief executive officer (CEO). But it's a mistake to think CEOs control big companies. This may be true as a practical matter in companies where the CEO also controls a majority of the company's voting shares. Outside that context, executives are hired hands who serve at the board's pleasure. The public may think the CEO rules the company, just as the residents of the City of Oz believed they were ruled by a gigantic floating green head. But the real power lies with the men and women behind the curtain—the board. Even the most charismatic CEO can suddenly find himself or herself out of a job, as shown by Steve Jobs' 1985 departure from Apple, Martha Stewart's 2003 indictment-triggered resignation from Martha Stewart Living, and Travis Kalanick's recent ouster from Uber's corner office.

So, if directors enjoy enormous control over and responsibility for companies but are not lavishly paid and are barred by the fiduciary duty of loyalty from using their positions for personal profit, why would anyone want to be a director? The answer surely varies from director to director, and there's little good data available. But status and reputation seem to provide the answers. Corporate directors tend to be older and well established. Many are retired CEOs, politicians, or public figures who are already wealthy. These individuals view a position on the board of a large company as an honor and an attractive part-time capstone to their careers.

Does it make sense to put these people in charge of such enormously powerful institutions? It depends on your vantage point, but the proof is in the pudding. Board governance has stood the test of time—directors have been successfully governing for-profit and nonprofit corporations for centuries, indeed for as long as there have been corporations. Certainly there have been problems with particular boards at particular companies at particular times. But the system has worked well enough that corporate entities have survived, thrived, and done great things for humanity for centuries. And, in cases where things go wrong with the board, there's another group that can weigh in and discipline dysfunctional or dishonest directors: the company's shareholders.

Player 3: The Shareholders

As noted above, shareholders don't own companies, but they do own shares of stock. Stock can be thought of as a kind of contract between the corporate entity and the shareholder that gives the shareholder two important rights. The first is the economic right to receive dividends—if, and only if, the board of directors declares some. The second right is the political right to vote on certain extremely limited matters. These include the right to veto certain mergers if the board proposes them, and the right to make shareholder "proposals." Although shareholder proposals often draw a lot of media attention, boards have significant leeway in deciding whether to exclude them, and as a practical matter they have not provided much of a check on the corporate system. Real shareholder political power lies in a third matter the law gives shareholders: *the right to determine who serves on the company's board of directors.*

This is a powerful political right indeed. But, as we are about to see, many shareholders are not particularly interested in using it. They don't buy stock to play a role in corporate governance; they buy hoping to sell to someone else at a higher price.

Shareholders themselves are often divided into two broad categories: individual (retail) shareholders and institutional shareholders. Individual shareholders are just that—people who buy and hold shares in their own names, usually for some goal like saving to retire, to buy a house, or to pay a child's college tuition. Although the number has been declining, today individual shareholders still directly own approximately 30 percent of shares of US public companies.[2]

The other important category of shareholders is institutional shareholders. Institutional shareholders account for approximately 70 percent of the market.[3] This label is commonly applied to mutual funds, pension funds, and other "pooled investment vehicles" (organizations created to allow investors to pool their funds and put them under the control of professional managers who invest and manage them collectively on the investors' behalf). Mutual funds and pension funds are supposed to be run not for the benefit of their fund managers but for the benefit of the fund's "beneficiaries"—the mutual fund's investors, and the employees and retirees with interests in the pension funds. These beneficiaries are said to invest "indirectly," leaving it up to their fund managers to decide which stocks to buy or sell and whether to reinvest or distribute dividends or trading profits earned by the fund portfolio. They also, critically, leave it up to their fund managers to decide whether and how to vote the portfolio's shares.

On first inspection, the politics of US shareholding looks reasonably democratic. In theory, directors control corporations, and shareholders elect (or potentially, could elect) directors. Moreover, about half of American adults own stock, either directly or through their interests in pension or mutual funds.[4] It would be nice to think our corporations were dedicated to serving the interests of at least that half—including their interests as customers, employees, taxpayers, and human beings who care about their fellow citizens and their descendants.

However, when we look below the surface, things become more complicated. Fewer and fewer Americans are investing. In 2008, 62 percent were in the market. Today that figure hovers around 54 percent.[5] Moreover, stock holdings are concentrated among the old, the white, and the wealthy. Nearly two-thirds of Americans ages 50–64 invest in equities, but less than one-third of those 18–29 do, and the percentage of young adults in the market is declining.[6] Share ownership also is skewed by race. In 2011, African Americans had a median liquid wealth of $200, including both checking and retirement accounts, while whites had a median liquid wealth of $23,000.[7] Finally, the top 10 percent of American wealth holders hold more than 90 percent of shares (and the share votes that go with them).[8]

When shareholders are mostly rich, white, and old, we shouldn't be surprised if they elect directors who look much the same and tend to run companies in ways that serve these groups' interests. But the problem of unequal shareholder influence due to biased stock ownership pales in comparison to a more extreme distortion in power over corporate boards. The most influential group in the boardroom today isn't a shareholder group at all. It's *fund managers*—and they may have little reason to pay attention to the needs, desires, or welfare of average shareholders, much less average citizens.

The simple truth is that power over the American corporate sector has been concentrated in the hands of few because *most shareholders don't vote.*

Shareholders Who Own Stock Directly Don't Vote (and Those Who Own Indirectly Can't)

To understand the dysfunctions driving American companies today, it is critical to first understand that most shareholders who own stock directly don't vote.[9] As economists put it, shareholders are "rationally apathetic." They know voting—even "proxy" voting by mail, phone, or online—demands time and attention. And, because the average individual shareholder owns only a small fraction of the shares of a single company, they also understand their vote is unlikely to affect the outcome. So they prefer to free ride on the votes of other investors. Only shareholders who own enough stock to make a difference—for example, "controlling" shareholders, like Walmart's Walton family—have reason to vote. For the rest of shareholders, voting is a costly and purely symbolic act. No wonder that when the 2016 corporate election season came around, only 28 percent of shares owned directly by individuals were voted[10] (most, presumably, by wealthy shareholders with large-enough stakes that their vote might be controlling). The other 72 percent of individual investors' ballots ended up in the physical or electronic trash.[11]

What about investors who hold stocks through their interests in pension and mutual funds? Like shareholders who own directly, these indirect investors don't have much reason to care about voting. But, instead of throwing their ballots into the trash, they delegate their voting rights to the manager who runs their fund. Indirect investors are often completely disengaged—they let their portfolio managers vote for them.

For much the same reasons as for individual investors, fund managers also don't have much interest in voting—careful voting takes a lot of time and attention, especially if you are managing a portfolio of fifty, one hundred, or even more stocks. And because even a large mutual or pension fund typically owns only a small fraction of any single company's shares, again the fund manager's vote is unlikely to make a difference. If a portfolio manager thinks a company's board is doing a bad job, the easiest solution is to do the "Wall Street Walk" by selling the shares as quickly and quietly as possible, before other investors see the problem and the price drops.

But federal regulations pressure mutual and pension fund managers to vote the shares of the stocks in their portfolios anyway.[12] By itself, this may be a good thing; without these rules, the typical public company director election might be a collective shareholder "no-show." (Corporations still have such difficulty getting a quorum of shares to cast votes that there are specialty businesses to help them do this.) However, it has also perversely distorted our corporate governance system. Individual shareholders mostly don't vote, but fund managers *vote more than 90 percent of the shares they control.*[13] Fund managers have become far and away the most powerful force in director elections in companies that don't have a controlling shareholder. It is fund managers that directors care about and listen to most closely—not the fund investors and pension beneficiaries whom they are supposed to represent, nor the individual shareholders who still own the largest single chunk of the market, and certainly not average Americans.

Player 4: Fund Portfolio Managers

So, if we want to understand who really controls corporations, we need to understand fund managers and what makes them tick. This is important, because the interests of fund managers and the interests of individual investors, and even the interests of fund managers and the fund investors and beneficiaries they supposedly represent, may be different.

Most individuals who invest in the stock market—whether directly or indirectly through a fund—have long-term goals in mind. Again, this might be saving for retirement, buying a home, or paying for a child's college tuition. Fund managers, however, are usually evaluated and compensated according to how their portfolios have performed in the last few quarters or at most the last few years. They have little room to think about the long term. The manager whose portfolio underperforms the market for four quarters risks being called on the carpet or even canned.[14]

And fund managers have even less room to think about how the companies in their portfolios are performing in terms of how they treat their employees, the quality of their products, their environmental responsibility, paying their fair share of taxes, and so forth. Fund managers' education, training, culture, and especially their compensation plans drive them to define "performance" in terms of how much the value of the portfolios they manage has risen or declined after taking account of cash received from dividends and share repurchases, trading profits from buying and selling, and how much the market prices of the shares in the portfolio have risen or fallen over the past year or so.[15]

The result is a deep divide—one might even say a chasm—between the personal interests of fund managers and the interests of average citizens who invest in funds (not to mention future generations and the planet). This divide is the source of many of the economic, social, and ethical problems we see in how corporations operate today.[16] It is reinforced and widened even further by the activities of proxy advisory services and hedge funds.

Player 5: Shareholder Proxy Advisory Services

The fifth important group that plays a critical role in corporate governance today is a type of business most readers have never heard of: shareholder proxy advisory services. Because companies may have hundreds of thousands or even millions of shareholders—far too many to bring together in one place at one time—corporate elections for boards of directors are typically held by "proxy," i.e., shareholders don't vote in person but instead send their votes in by mail or electronically. For an institutional investor overseeing a portfolio that includes the stocks of dozens or even hundreds of companies, casting all those votes is a burdensome chore. In the past, fund managers, like individual shareholders, often either didn't bother to vote or routinely cast their votes to support incumbent boards. However, federal regulations passed in the past few decades have put increasing pressure on fund managers to vote their shares and to explain their voting policies to their investors.[17] Most have responded by outsourcing the whole messy business of proxy voting to for-profit businesses known as proxy advisory services.

Proxy advisory firms play a powerful role in corporate elections today. For a modest fee, proxy advisors issue guidance on how to vote the stocks in the fund manager's portfolio and will even do the job of actually casting the votes. The largest player in the industry is Institutional Shareholder Services (ISS), followed by Glass Lewis. In 2007, the US Government Accountability Office (GAO) estimated that ISS advised institutional clients holding *$25 trillion* in assets. Runner-up Glass Lewis is estimated to advise clients holding $15 trillion.[18] Together, it is estimated that ISS and Glass Lewis comprise 97 percent of the total market for proxy services to institutional investors. In other words, these two businesses advise and cast the votes for the vast majority of pension and mutual funds—and those pension and mutual funds control the vast majority of shares cast in director elections in large public companies. In mid-cap and large US companies, ISS alone has been estimated to cast 25 to 50 percent of all shares voted.[19]

Many pension and mutual funds assert that they exercise independent oversight on how the shares of the companies in their portfolios are voted and that they don't routinely vote as ISS or Glass Lewis advise. Yet companies certainly act as if they think the proxy advisory industry's guidelines have influence. A 2012 survey, for example, found that 70 percent of corporate directors and executives who responded reported that they took proxy advisory firms' policies into account when making their own decisions regarding executive compensation.[20] A recent 2016 report from the GAO found similar results.[21]

Proxy advisors operate in the background, but they are incredibly important players in the modern corporate governance game. Their voting recommendations impact the outcome of many corporate contests, especially in companies that don't have a controlling shareholder with enough voting power to control the outcome. Boards of directors have become exquisitely sensitive to what the proxy services say about how companies ought to be run. Does ISS recommend the board sell the company to a possible acquirer? Directors know that if they disagree, they may find themselves on the losing side of a proxy battle in the next annual election. Does Glass Lewis recommend the CEO be compensated with stock options? Many boards today are happy to oblige.

This brings us to the sixth group in our corporate governance system—hedge funds.

Player 6: Hedge Funds (the Consummate Short-Term Investors)

Hedge funds are a bit like mutual funds in that they bring together different investors' assets to be collectively invested by professional managers. Unlike mutual funds, however, hedge funds are very lightly regulated. Only wealthy individuals and institutions like universities and pension funds are allowed to invest in them. (Yes, pension funds can pass the job of managing their beneficiaries' assets on to hedge funds.)

Hedge fund managers typically are paid only if their investments have positive returns. Moreover, although they don't allow their investors to demand their money back immediately, the typical investor "lock-up" period is only one or two years. Hedge fund managers accordingly are under tremendous pressure to produce profits quickly. If they don't, they don't get paid, and their fund is likely to fail.[22]

One kind of hedge fund, the activist fund, has learned how to take advantage of today's corporate governance system—often at the expense of other investors, corporations, and society. Activist funds typically hold investments for an average of two years or less.[23] One of their strategies is to acquire a block of a company's shares (typically 5 percent or less), then launch a publicity campaign targeting the company's directors and executives (often intended to shame and/or embarrass them). The campaign is then typically followed by threatening a proxy contest to replace members of the board who don't agree with the hedge fund's proposed strategy. Such strategies tend to be couched in terms that urge the company to pursue corporate policies to "unlock shareholder value" by quickly raising share price, for example, or by repurchasing shares, divesting assets, or cutting payroll and research and development. If the board agrees and the share price rises, the hedge fund sells and gets out.

Boards know that even though an activist may only own a small percentage of the company's shares, hedge funds often form "wolf packs" that work together. Moreover, once an activist campaign has begun, the activists' ideas are likely to get the support of the proxy advisors—and with it, the votes of the fund managers who play such an outsized role in corporate elections. Boards accordingly fear and loathe activists, and dread being targeted by them. They often give in to activists' demands, and companies that haven't yet been targeted adopt similar strategies to keep share price high and discourage activists from showing up in the first place.

In 2016, activist funds collectively controlled only about $110 billion in assets.[24] This is a drop in the corporate bucket compared to the US stock market's total capitalization of around $30 trillion. Yet they have become enormously influential in corporate director elections, launching campaigns against the directors of nearly 10 percent of public companies each year and targeting ever-larger firms.

Let us see how this all plays out by looking at the case of ValueAct Capital and Valeant Pharmaceuticals, which illustrates the interaction among the six players in the corporate governance system that create a short-termism feedback loop.

Case Study 3: Valeant and ValueAct

ValueAct is a hedge fund. In 2006, it invested $200 million in Valeant Pharmaceuticals, then a relatively small company.[25] A ValueAct representative was given a seat on the Valeant board. At his suggestion, the company hired a new CEO, Mike Pearson, and gave him a compensation contract that rewarded him handsomely if he could deliver "45% annual compounded returns over a three-year period."[26]

That's just what Pearson set out to do. He began by buying Canadian company Biovail in 2010, which allowed Valeant to do a tax "inversion" and become a Canadian company, which in turn allowed Valeant to avoid paying US taxes.[27] Pearson then started borrowing large amounts to fund other acquisitions. Typically, when Valeant acquired a target it would announce massive layoffs: 1,100 jobs at Biovail, up to 2,700 at Bausch & Lomb, 260 at Salix, 77 at small Dendreon.[28] It would slash investments in research and development. Where traditional big drug companies spent 15 to 20 percent of sales on researching and developing new drugs, Valeant spent only 3 percent.[29] And it pursued what would eventually become a controversial strategy: fueling profits by raising the price of essential medicines as high as the market would bear.

In the name of its "duty to shareholders," in 2013 Valeant acquired two lifesaving heart drugs from Marathon Pharmaceuticals: Isuprel and Nitropress. It then raised their prices *525 percent* and *212 percent*. It also raised the price of two other drugs it acquired that are used to treat the rare and potentially fatal condition Wilson's disease from about $500 to about $24,000 for a thirty-day supply.[30]

But eventually, problems began to surface at the company. In 2016 the Securities and Exchange Commission (SEC) began investigating its financial statements and its relationship with a mail-order pharmacy it controlled, and the Justice Department began looking at its drug pricing practices and allegations of possible health care fraud at its Bausch & Lomb unit.[31] Between August of 2015 and March

2016, Valeant's stock price fell more than 80 percent, from a high of $262.5 to $33 per share.[32] Pearson was removed as CEO and replaced by his former hedge fund buddy, Bill Ackman. Today, Valeant remains a shadow of its former self.

At the time, billionaire Warren Buffett's longtime partner Charlie Munger had described Valeant's strategy as "deeply immoral."[33] But the online magazine *Canadian Business* named Pearson "2015 CEO of the Year." [34] And hedge funds and mutual funds started viewing Valeant as a stock to buy.[35]

ISS (one of the proxy advisors) loved Valeant, too. When Valeant made an unsuccessful attempt to acquire Botox-maker Allergan in 2014, ISS recommended that Allergan's shareholders vote in favor of a special meeting to remove six of Allergan's directors, noting that "Valeant has [had] enormous success over the tenure of its current CEO."[36] The Allergan shareholders who favored Valeant included Bill Ackman's hedge fund, Pershing Square. Pershing had bought 10 percent of Allergan's shares, and Ackman worked closely with Pearson to push the acquisition through presumably in the hope that Valeant would buy Allergan and pay a hefty premium. Pershing and Valeant recently agreed to pay $290 million to settle insider trading claims brought against them by other Allergan shareholders.[37] As far as ISS was concerned, Pearson's dedication to raising Valeant's share price by any means possible was an exemplary case of "good corporate governance."

ISS's embrace of "shareholder value" as Valeant's corporate objective did more than help Pearson harm Valeant, however. Because so many mutual and pension fund managers follow the proxy services' voting guidelines, and seem to vote in lockstep according to those guidelines, corporate directors and executives fixate on the guidelines, too—including corporate directors and executives in the drug industry. The proxy services' support for Pearson and Valeant ended up shifting the direction of the entire pharmaceuticals business.

Rationally anticipating that they might be the targets of the next activist campaign, the boards of other drug companies began following Pearson's and Valeant's playbook. Many pursued tax inversions and became foreign companies to reduce their US tax bills. Others embraced Valeant's practices of firing employees, cutting research and development, and raising drug prices to unsustainable levels in the quest for short-term profits. When Turing Pharmaceuticals was acquired by former hedge fund manager Martin Shkreli, it promptly raised the price of a toxoplasmosis drug critical to AIDS patients from $13.50 a pill to $750.[38] Mylan provoked widespread public outrage when it raised the price of the EpiPens highly allergic children carry to school from about $100 to more than $600.[39]

The proxy services' institutional voting guidelines for the pharmaceutical industry thus (perhaps unwittingly) ended up rubber-stamping practices that harmed innumerable customers, employees, long-term shareholders, and taxpayers—not to mention future generations who look to the industry to develop lifesaving drugs and medical treatments. Although ValueAct eventually made more than $1 billion profit on its investment in Valeant before it sold, the company's share price has not recovered. Similarly, Mylan's EpiPen is rapidly losing market share to cheaper generics devised by competitors.[40]

Can the System Fix Itself?

Unequal share ownership, even more unequal shareholder voting power, skewed incentives, the capture of entire industries by unaccountable hedge funds, and the replication (again perhaps unwittingly) of these tendencies in proxy service guidelines leaves us with a current system of corporate governance that is lopsided, broken, and dysfunctional. It places control over many of our biggest and most economically important companies in the hands of a small group of individuals and institutions who wield grossly outsized influence and whose incentives oftentimes drive them to single-mindedly seek short-term share price gains while ignoring harmful consequences to other investors, stakeholders, the environment, and even the company's own future.

Is there any hope the system can fix itself? (Or would free markets fix the system?) Two trends are worth mentioning. The first is the rise of "indexed" mutual funds that buy and hold shares in the stocks that make up a particular index, like the S&P 500 or the Russell 2000. Index funds and a variant on them, the exchange-traded fund or ETF, are of necessity long-term "passive" shareholders; they can't do the Wall Street Walk that active fund managers are so fond of. As a result, their portfolio managers' interests may be more closely aligned with those of longer-term investors.

In practice, two factors work against this. First, index funds have little incentive to challenge corporate policies that emphasize profits over concerns like employee welfare or environmental quality. Second, even a large index fund typically holds only a small percentage of the shares in any particular company. This makes index fund managers subject to the same rational apathy that discourages other noncontrolling shareholders from paying attention to corporate governance. Not surprisingly, many index funds also turn to proxy advisors for help in voting guidance and logistics.[41]

The second trend may have far greater impact, for good or for ill. Many businesspeople recognize the current governance system makes it difficult or impossible to run a public company in a sustainable, responsible fashion. In response, they are taking steps to avoid being enmeshed in the governance system we've described. Where once company founders eagerly looked forward to "going public" and acquiring outside shareholders, many entrepreneurs now dread this. Uber, SpaceX, Pinterest, WeWork, and Airbnb have all chosen to remain private companies. Meanwhile, founders and managers of other public companies have bought out their public shareholders and "gone private," as Michael Dell did when he took data storage provider EMC private.

And the founders and management teams of companies that do go public are increasingly adopting a clever strategy to ensure control remains in their hands: issuing two or more "classes" of shares. The share class sold to the public has weak voting rights—say, one vote per share (or in the case of Snapchat, no votes per share)—while the class issued to founders and managers has stronger rights (e.g., ten votes per share). Google, Alphabet, and Facebook—not to mention the early example of Warren Buffett and Charlie Munger's famed and highly successful investment firm Berkshire Hathaway—are all seemingly public companies that are actually controlled by a handful of individuals.

Corporate America's collective move away from market pressure may have social benefits. Companies insulated from the demands of short-term hedge fund activists and mutual fund managers have more freedom to pursue long-term, innovative research projects. Alphabet is working on developing self-driving cars; SpaceX on commercial space travel. Founders and managers also have good reason to spend substantial time and energy understanding a company's business and tend to be longer-term investors who aren't interested in sacrificing the company's future just to temporarily boost share price. Having created and nurtured their companies, they are more likely to be concerned about, and even take pride in, the quality of its products, the welfare of its employees, and its public reputation. Of course there is no guarantee that a company's managers and founders will care how their company impacts society. But if they do care, they have more breathing room to act on their concern.

Yet there is a dark side to the trend. Individuals have amassed great fortunes creating companies that they still control. Prominent examples include Jeff Bezos at Amazon, Mark Zuckerberg at Facebook, the Walton family at Walmart, Elon Musk at Tesla and SpaceX, and Charles and David Koch at Koch Industries. They can use their economic power to seek political or cultural power: consider Bezos's purchase of the *Washington Post*, or the Koch-funded political advocacy group Americans for Prosperity. Meanwhile, public participation in the stock market is declining, and the number of public companies in which average Americans can invest has been cut by more than half over the past two decades, from approximately 7,500 to approximately 3,500.[42] We are seeing the rise of a small, enormously powerful, and unaccountable elite of controlling shareholders who not only enjoy the lion's share of the financial wealth generated by the businesses that drive our economy—they control these powerful, pervasive entities as well.

From Ancient Rome, to eighteenth-century France, to Russia in 1917, to many modern Arab states, history has shown that societies dominated by small, wealthy elites fare poorly. They may end with a bang (revolution and revolt) or they may end with a whimper (slow stagnation). But the end is rarely pretty. Is the United States destined to become a hereditary plutocracy? Such a future does not mesh with American heritage, values, or aspirations.

Thus, how can we address the flaws in the corporate governance system?

Author Lynn Stout repeatedly pointed out how any attempt to fix the system requires a bit of "corporate jujitsu." Finding the right leverage points and points of attack are key to redirecting the behavior and outcomes of the system. The Universal Fund offers such an intervention.

Chapter 3

Introducing the
Universal Fund

The Universal Fund we envision (we will call it the Fund, with a capital "F") in many ways resembles a typical mutual fund—ultimately, we hope, a very large one. Mutual funds are a type of "pooled investment vehicle" that brings together money or other valuable assets from many different investors so it can be invested collectively. The typical mutual fund is organized as a company with shareholders. (Mutual funds are also called investment companies. However, where other companies produce and sell cars, software, or shampoo, the business of a mutual fund or other pooled investment vehicle is to hold investments, often in other companies that do sell cars, software, or shampoo.) Like a standard mutual fund, the Universal Fund we propose would hold an investment portfolio. The assets in this portfolio would consist mostly of stocks of public and private companies. But the Universal Fund could also hold small amounts of bonds, cash, or other assets.

1. A Universal Fund for All Citizens

As in the case of a typical mutual fund, the Universal Fund would have shareholders. But these shareholders would not be limited to the relatively wealthy, self-selected investors who pay to purchase shares, as with a typical stock investment.

Citizen-share ownership would be a privilege available to every US citizen eighteen or older who goes to the trouble of registering to become a citizen-shareholder,[1] just as the right to vote is a privilege available to any citizen who complies with the voter registration process. Of course, it would be possible to apply other criteria for becoming a citizen-shareholder. Citizen-shares could be made available to US citizens of any age, including minors, or to all legal residents of the US. Another possibility is that citizen-shares could be subject to "means testing" and distributed only to those who fall below certain income or wealth thresholds. While the precise design of the Fund would be determined by its founding funders, we do note that the decision to include a means test cuts against the goal of equal participation in the Fund by a broad range of citizens. As a default, our plan envisions all US citizens eighteen years or older being eligible to become citizen-shareholders. There are several reasons why we advocate this, but an especially important one is that our plan for Citizen Capitalism does more than equalize influence and income. It also seeks to reinvigorate civic society and encourage support for the capitalist system by empowering, engaging, and inspiring widespread citizen participation in the governance of our corporate sector.

The current proposal focuses on a Fund for United States citizens. Similar plans could easily be adopted by other nations: one could imagine an Italian Fund or a UK Fund. Other nations, such as Norway, Singapore, and Mexico, have already created state-owned "sovereign wealth funds" that invest on behalf of their citizens. So, it would not be surprising to see a foreign Fund created before one is created in the US. It is further possible to imagine Funds with a regional basis—a European Union Fund or a Caribbean Community (CARICOM) Fund, for example—or even a Global Universal Fund.

While sovereign wealth funds are close analogs to the Universal Fund, they differ in two key ways—sovereign wealth funds rely on government action to bring them into being, and they are typically funded by proceeds generated from natural resources, such as oil or mineral extraction. The Universal Fund is cut from a different cloth. It is a private ordering venture that does not necessitate government funding and relies entirely on the voluntary participation of willing funders and shareholders. The voluntary nature of our particular proposal for a privately created Fund is culturally and economically suited to the US. Moreover, for good or ill, many Americans identify with their nation and fellow citizens more closely and warmly than with the rest of the world. They are comfortable with programs like Social Security, Medicare, and K-12 public education, which equalize income and opportunity within US borders. Programs that move American resources abroad are more controversial.

2. Assets Acquired from Donations

Another key element of our proposal is that the Universal Fund would acquire the securities in its portfolio primarily from shares donated by companies and from donations by individuals, especially high-net-worth individuals. This is an important aspect of our plan, because it means *Citizen Capitalism does not rely on government funding.* It is a private ordering innovation that relies only on the *voluntary* actions of individuals and companies.

Several factors indicate that if a Universal Fund were created, donations would be likely. First, if legislation was passed making donations to the fund tax-deductible, donors could enjoy tax deductions.[2] This would be especially important for attracting corporate donations. Consider the fact that corporations already purchase $400 to $600 *billion* of their own shares every year. If those shares were donated to the Fund instead of retired, these corporations could claim tax deductions potentially worth $100 billion or more annually.

Second, even if donations to the Fund were not tax-deductible, corporations that donate would still be perceived as more socially responsible. It is hard to imagine a more effective way for a company to signal its interest in benefiting society and the nation than by donating some of its shares to the Universal Fund. Donations to the Fund would serve a signaling function that the donating corporation cares about broader societal interests, and this would particularly be the case for pioneer funders.

Individuals, too, have reasons to donate. This is especially true for the ultrawealthy. Consider the Giving Pledge for billionaires recently organized by Bill Gates and Warren Buffett. The Giving Pledge is a "commitment by the world's wealthiest individuals and families to dedicate the majority of their wealth to giving back."[3] At the time this book went to print, it had attracted 184 signatories from twenty-two countries, each of whom pledged to give away at least half of their wealth.[4]

Finally but critically, although the Fund initially may be small, it is structured to grow. Corporations and individuals will continue to make donations over time. Meanwhile, when citizen-shareholders die, their interest in their citizen-shares reverts to the Fund. This helps the Fund preserve its assets and allows it to issue new citizen-shares to US citizens who reach the age of eighteen without significantly diluting the value of existing citizen-shareholders' interests. The Universal Fund will snowball, continually increasing in size until it ultimately provides citizen-shareholders with both a significant source of supplemental income and a personal stake in our capitalist corporate system.

3. Pass-Through of Portfolio Income to Citizen-Shareholders

Like the investment portfolio of a typical mutual fund, the Universal Fund portfolio would generate income. This income would come mostly from the dividends declared by the companies whose shares are held by the Universal Fund, along with cash received from corporate share repurchases and interest payments from any bonds or other debt instruments it owns. And, like a typical mutual fund, it would "pass through" this income to its citizen-shareholders.

For example, after the Fund receives enough donations to reach some predetermined starting threshold—say, a $3 trillion portfolio—it would start to distribute all portfolio income to its citizen-shareholders on a periodic, proportionate basis. For example, assuming that the stocks in the portfolio yield dividends amounting to 2.25 percent annually on a $3 trillion portfolio, and that approximately 225 million Americans would qualify for and actually become citizen-shareholders, the Fund would generate *per capita* income of $300 annually for every American citizen who registers. But if only a portion of the eligible citizens registered for Citizen Capitalism, the annual income that each citizen-shareholder receives could be more significant.

This means, most obviously, that the Fund would be an ongoing and growing source of income to citizen-shareholders, providing a stream of financial benefits throughout each citizen-shareholder's life, from age eighteen until death. Of course, the amount of income citizen-shareholders would receive each year from the Fund would vary. Relevant factors include both the size of the Fund and the size of the investment returns generated by the Fund portfolio. Both are likely to increase over time.

4. Citizen-Shares Cannot Be Traded, Gifted, or Bequeathed

Citizen-share ownership would be a privilege of US citizens that cannot be bought or sold, any more than the right to vote can be bought or sold. As legal experts put it, citizen-share ownership would be an "inalienable" right.[5] It could be decided that the privilege of citizen-share ownership should be revoked in certain circumstances, just as the right to vote can be revoked. But as a general rule, each citizen is allowed to hold one and only one citizen-share. Moreover, citizen-shares are held for life and cannot be sold or traded away. Upon the death of a citizen-shareholder, their citizen-share would revert to the Fund (thus marginally increasing the value of all other citizen-shareholders' interests in the Fund portfolio, just as the issuance of new citizen-shares to new citizen-shareholders would marginally dilute all other citizen-shareholders' interests). Similarly, citizen-shareholders are not allowed to trade away the rights that come with citizen-share ownership. They could not, for example, use their citizen-shares as collateral to borrow money or enter "derivative" contracts that require them to make payments based on the income a citizen-shareholder receives from a citizen-share.

The potential problem of trading away citizen-shares or the rights that come with them could be addressed by making contracts to sell shares or the rights that accompany shares legally unenforceable, meaning the contracts cannot be enforced in court. This is not as radical an idea as it may sound. Many types of sales are legally unenforceable—for example, you can't enforce a contract to buy someone's vote in a political election. Making a contract of sale for something legally unenforceable can be a highly effective way of discouraging trading in that something, especially when the contract requires the something to be delivered in the future. Most buyers would not likely want to pay good money for the right to receive income from a citizen-share if they can't be sure that, when the time comes, the selling citizen-shareholder has to deliver the income.

Gifts or inheritances of citizen-shares also would not be allowed. This does not mean that citizen-shareholders could not use the money they have received in any way they want—if they decide to give their earned dividends away to family or friends, that is their choice and prerogative. Upon a citizen-shareholders' death, however, their citizen-share reverts to the Fund. Meanwhile, corporations and individuals will continue to make donations over time. The net effect is that although the Fund initially may be relatively small, it is structured to grow over time. The portfolio is like a lobster trap—assets go in, but they can't come out. This helps the Fund preserve its assets while issuing citizen-shares to new citizen-shareholders. The Universal Fund is designed to grow in size until it ultimately provides each citizen-shareholder with a meaningful return and consequently a significant personal investment in the corporate sector and our capitalist system.

Importantly, it also means the sole economic benefit enjoyed by citizen-shareholders by virtue of their interest in the Fund would be a proportionate interest in the income the Fund generated from its portfolio of stocks. Citizen-shareholders of necessity are long-term investors.[6] Nor is their income from their share guaranteed. Rather, it would be determined by the long-term performance and distribution policies of the underlying corporations whose stocks were held in the portfolio—giving citizen-shareholders an ongoing economic interest in the health of the US economy and the corporate sector.

5. Fund Administrators Cannot Trade and Have Limited Discretion

Under our proposal, the Fund would be run by professionals whom we call administrators, who would be tasked with executing only limited, predetermined functions. Their duties and compensation would look very different from the duties and compensation of most mutual and pension fund managers today.

The Fund would be carefully and deliberately structured to minimize the risk that administrators might use it to pursue personal agendas. This starts with their compensation. Fund administrators would receive a fixed fee for performing limited, predetermined tasks. This means, for example, administrators' compensation must be unrelated to either the assets in, or the income generated by, the Fund portfolio. They would not have any financial interest in trying to inflate either the portfolio's size or its returns. This avoids the perverse short-term incentives discussed in chapter 2, which can distort the behavior of so many mutual and pension fund managers today.

Similarly, the procedures for selecting and retaining Fund administrators would be chosen to keep them independent, ethical, and dedicated to authentically representing citizen-shareholders' interests. For example, administrators could be periodically elected by citizen-shareholders, drawn at random from the citizenry as jurors are chosen, and/or selected to represent certain demographics. They might also be subject to meeting minimal qualifications, term limits, or age requirements. These need not be conventional age requirements; there might be advantages, for example, to requiring a certain percentage of administrators to be between the ages of eighteen and thirty, and another percentage over sixty. Administrators could also be removed for unethical or inappropriate behavior. And, the Fund would be structured to be as transparent as possible: financial statements; administrators' identities, backgrounds, and potential conflicts of interest; and fund decision-making processes would all be disclosed and available for public inspection.

Finally, Fund administrators would *not* be given discretion to buy and sell assets in the Fund portfolio in an effort to reap trading profits by "beating the market." Assets would enter the portfolio only through donations and exit only through transactions initiated and controlled by third parties (for example, a merger agreement requiring the portfolio to exchange shares it holds for shares in another company or for cash). Should the Fund find itself with too much cash or other non-stock assets in its portfolio, Fund administrators would be directed to convert these assets to stocks through some neutral trading rule like "purchase a proportionate amount of all the stocks in the S&P 500" or "purchase the stocks already held by the portfolio." In other words, the administrators' job would be just that—passive administration, including such activities as maintaining a list of citizen-shareholders and periodically distributing income from the portfolio.

Citizen Capitalism's overall approach of relying on passive administrators to manage the Fund and its portfolio generates one last and substantial advantage: it ensures that administrators' fees should be quite low. As we propose it, the administrators' job is even more limited than the tasks done today by the "passive" index mutual fund managers that do not trade but simply buy and hold the stocks listed in a particular index like the S&P 500. Index funds typically charge their shareholders extremely low fees. Indeed, the fees are so low they are typically measured in "basis points" (a basis point is 1/100th of 1 percent). Vanguard and Charles Schwab, for example, offer exchange-traded funds (ETFs)—a kind of index fund that are like mutual funds but trade like stocks—that charge management fees of only 3 to 5 basis points annually. Similarly low expenses would be associated with administering the Universal Fund.[7]

6. Citizen-Shareholders Determine How the Portfolio Votes Its Shares

Finally, we come to a critical component of our plan that distinguishes it from the typical Universal Basic Income (UBI) or wealth redistribution proposals. Under Citizen Capitalism, citizen-shareholders would receive more than just an economic right to an equal share of the income paid to the portfolio. They would also receive a proportionate *political* right to vote the stocks held in the portfolio in shareholder meetings. Our plan would give citizen-shareholders a powerful voice in corporate governance—and importantly, it would be a diversified, human voice.

We fully recognize that, without more incentive, few individual citizen-shareholders would bother informing themselves about what's going on in the companies whose shares are held in the portfolio, or even with voting their shares. Good corporate governance is a shared or "common" good that, as every beginning economics student soon learns, tends to be under-provided. Shareholders know the time, effort, and resources they put into becoming informed and voting in corporate elections are costs they bear alone. Meanwhile, the benefits of better long-term corporate returns and more responsible corporate behavior are shared by all. They also understand that the odds of their individual vote making a difference are slim to none. Our plan is designed to counter these patterns. It not only gives citizen-shareholders an interest in corporate stocks, it also allows them to easily vote those stocks in corporate elections in a collective and informed fashion by using a qualified proxy advisor.

A well-designed proxy advisory service could go a long way to overcoming this apathy. As we saw in the previous chapter, proxy advisory services exist today. They research companies, develop guidelines for casting votes in corporate elections, and actually cast the votes of the vast majority of shares held by mutual and pension funds. However, these services are not currently available to individual investors. Moreover, as discussed, proxy advisory services in many ways reinforce existing patterns in the corporate governance system. As a reminder, the vast majority of individuals who own stock directly don't bother to vote, while those who invest through mutual or pension funds delegate the unwelcome task of share voting to their fund managers. Fund managers, in turn, typically care only about buying a stock whose price will soon rise so they can sell and make a quick profit—preferably, by tomorrow. They may or may not particularly care about the company's impact on other companies, on long-term profits, on customers or employees, on society, or on future generations.

Having the Fund approve and pay for any qualified proxy service used by citizen-shareholders would create incentives for the development of new proxy services that cater to the authentic interests of long-term, diversified, socially concerned citizen-shareholders. In fact, the one exception to Fund administrators having no discretion could be that they would be given the power to set requirements for the proxy advisory services retained by citizen-shareholders, as well as the discretion to decide what fees the proxy services could charge. This is an important exception because the manner in which citizen-shares are voted should match the long-term perspective of the Fund. Proxy services are a key part of this puzzle. The proxy services we want to serve citizen-shareholders would have to be organized as nonprofits, completely transparent, and free from significant conflicts of interest, and their fees would have to be paid only by the Fund. Setting the fees to be paid to the services requires a bit more discretion, but provided the Fund administrators are carefully selected, compensated, and required to use fair and transparent decision-making processes, they would have little room to run amok.

In this chapter, we have laid out the bare bones of our proposal for the creation of a Universal Fund that is explicitly designed to equalize participation in capital markets, provide a counterweight to short-termism, and offer a stream of returns to participating citizen-shareholders. In the next chapter, we explain why we believe the Fund can be successfully funded by relying on private donations from both corporations and individuals.

Chapter 4

The Private Money Is There

One concern some may have about the feasibility of Citizen Capitalism is whether it's possible to raise enough assets through private donations to create a Fund with significant impact. Even a cursory inspection shows there is more than enough individual and corporate money available. Starting first with individuals, the Center on Wealth and Philanthropy at Boston College has predicted that by 2061, more than *$58 trillion* will be transferred from American estates, with nearly half of that amount ($27 trillion) going to charity.[1] Corporations, too, routinely spend substantial amounts that could be allocated to the Universal Fund. Although direct corporate philanthropy is relatively modest, corporations spend hundreds of billions of dollars in cash each year repurchasing shares from their own shareholders. These repurchased shares, which are then retired, could just as easily be donated to the Universal Fund. For the past five years, for example, the companies in the S&P 500 have typically averaged between $400 billion and $650 billion of total share repurchases annually—and peaked over $750 billion in the first 2018 quarter.[2] This figure does not include share repurchases by smaller public companies outside the S&P 500, or repurchases by private companies.

On the face of it there is more than enough individual and corporate money due to change hands in coming years to create a Universal Fund that would soon have assets in the trillions, or tens of trillions, of dollars. Is that sufficient? Let us do some quick calculations. The Census Bureau estimates there are about 227 million US citizens age eighteen or older. So, assuming some fluctuations in the number of citizens, let us estimate that 225 million would be eligible citizen-shareholders.[3]

Although the dividends that corporations pay shareholders vary from year to year, industry to industry, and company to company, as a historical matter the dividend yield on stocks (the ratio between the dividend a company pays and the market price of one of its shares) has typically fallen between 2 and 5 percent annually.[4] If we assume a dividend yield of 2.25 percent for the stocks in the Fund portfolio, this would mean a $1 trillion Fund would generate $100 annually for every citizen-shareholder, a $10 trillion Fund would generate $1,000, a $30 trillion Fund would generate $3,000, and so forth. By way of comparison, after starting small, the Alaska Permanent Fund pays dividends of $1,000–$2,000 today. It has proven itself one of the most popular policies in Alaskan history and has been estimated to reduce the state's poverty rate by 25 percent.[5]

Again, our figures are conservative. Given the relatively small amounts of income initially available, it's unlikely all eligible US citizens would immediately register to become citizen-shareholders. So let us assume that only 100 million out of the 227 million eligible US citizens sign up to become citizen-shareholders. Holding everything else constant, a $1 trillion fund would generate approximately $225 annually for every citizen-shareholder, a $10 trillion Fund would generate $2,250 annually, and a $30 trillion Fund would generate $6,750 for each citizen-shareholder. The absolute maximum the Fund could reach is boundless, particularly if, as we envision, the Fund was structured to allow donations of cash, equity, bonds, and other assets. Current US market capitalization stands at approximately $30 trillion, the US fixed income market is valued at more than $40 trillion, the REIT (real estate investment trust) market hit the $1 trillion mark in 2016, and sales in the US art market totaled approximately $22 billion in 2017.[6] Each of these segments of capital represents a source of potential donations to the Fund. As we are about to see, both individuals and corporations have good reasons to make donations in the next decade or two that could well exceed $10 trillion. Unlike the Alaska Permanent Fund, which is founded on a dwindling resource, the Fund is structured to grow indefinitely through ongoing donations. And if it improves long-term corporate performance, dividend yields would be even greater than our assumed 2.25 percent.

So the money is there. But what about the will?

Corporations Have Strong Motivations to Donate: Immediate Advantages

We begin by looking at corporations, because their motivations for donating shares are straightforward. Business corporations as a general rule don't spend much on charitable contributions. What they do spend enormous amounts of cash on—*$400 billion to $650 billion annually*—is buying back their own shares from their shareholders.[7] These corporate share repurchases provide a natural supply of stocks to be donated to the Universal Fund.

Why do companies spend so much money repurchasing their shares? The cash goes to shareholders and is the economic equivalent of a dividend. But share repurchases are perceived to help support share price.[8] They also satisfy, at least temporarily, hedge funds and mutual funds with short-term time horizons demanding an immediate return on their investments. With a share repurchase, the corporations' cash goes only to the short-term shareholders who already want out, in contrast to a dividend that would have to be paid to all shareholders.

What do companies do with the shares they repurchase? Essentially: nothing. Repurchased shares are relabeled "treasury" shares and can neither receive dividends nor be voted. In essence, the company spends an enormous amount of cash and gets in return a bit of relief from the pressures of short-term investors. If a company were to donate the shares it repurchases to the Universal Fund, it would still get this relief and it would secure a patient, long-term shareholder—the Fund. In addition, if donations to the Fund were made tax deductible, donating corporations would reap an immediate and substantial financial advantage: a tax deduction.[9]

Earning Customer, Employee, Community, and National Loyalty

Although harder to quantify, there is another important benefit a company would reap from donating repurchased shares. By doing so, it would earn the loyalty of up to roughly 225 million citizen-shareholders—citizen-shareholders who are also customers, employees, investors, taxpayers, and voters. This kind of loyalty is extremely valuable. To give just a few examples, it's common for today's consumers making purchases to consider not only the price and the quality of a good or service but also whether the business that provides it is socially and environmentally responsible. There are even mobile phone apps, like Good-Guide and Green Globe, to help them do so. Employees accept lower salaries to work at companies they perceive as more ethical. Investors who prefer socially responsible investing practices now comprise the fastest growing segment of the market for professional investment services.[10]

Companies recognize the economic benefits of being perceived as a "good corporate citizen." Some go to considerable lengths to develop this perception; companies like Costco, Starbucks, and Levi Strauss have deliberately positioned themselves in their media relations to appeal to consumers through this strategy. Other companies, like Patagonia and King Arthur Flour, have chosen to incorporate or reincorporate themselves as "benefit corporations" explicitly dedicated to pursuing social and environmental goals.[11] The first powerful institution to respond to the February 14, 2018, Parkland High School massacre perpetrated by a former student armed with a devastatingly lethal AR-15 semiautomatic rifle was not the Florida legislature. It was Dick's Sporting Goods. Dick's, which is one of the nation's leading gun sellers, announced early in the morning of February 28 that it was immediately ending sales of all assault-style rifles in its stores and raising the minimum age for all gun purchases to twenty-one.[12]

Moreover, many corporations, like Microsoft, Facebook, and Citigroup, have a foundation arm that focuses on philanthropic endeavors. For those corporate foundations focused on issues like economic progress or income inequality, donations to the Universal Fund could readily become part of their corporate philanthropic activities. In addition, for the hundreds of corporations that produce sustainability reports, like Coca-Cola or UPS, donations to the Universal Fund could be considered an extension of their approach to sustainability. Sustainability reports are stand-alone reports that are intended to describe the environmental, social, and financial impact of the company's activities, as well as demonstrate the connection between the company's strategy and its role in creating a sustainable economy.[13] In the United States, sustainability reporting is not mandatory. Yet in the past few years, the number of corporations that do sustainability reports has quadrupled from a mere 20 percent of the S&P 500 in 2011 to 82 percent of the index in 2016.[14] The uptick in sustainability reporting is part of a broader trend, which anecdotally demonstrates that the world of social concerns and the corporate world are moving closer together. Other aspects of this trend include the rise of new corporate forms such as "benefit corporations" or "social purpose corporations," which are explicitly formed to pursue both financial and social value creation; the establishment of social stock exchanges, which are only available to corporations that commit to returning both financial and social value; and numerous studies that repeatedly show that millennials want to work for companies that demonstrate values and ethics. The Universal Fund can be viewed as being synergistically aligned with this wider sustainability movement. Corporate donations to the Universal Fund are an efficient and relatively painless way for a company to affirmatively demonstrate its commitment to sustainability and a certain set of social values and ethics. Finally, many corporations might see the Universal Fund as a desirable long-term shareholder that would support management decisions to reinvest and to take care of stakeholders like employees and customers.

In suggesting that companies have strong financial reasons to pay attention to how the public perceives them, we do not mean to cynically suggest that the employees, managers, and directors of these companies do not care about the public welfare. To the contrary, we believe many of them care deeply. The difficulty they face is that, in a system structured to focus them on raising share price, it can be hard to incorporate such concerns unless they are tied to a plausible long-term benefit for the company. Because donating shares to the Universal Fund would help a company appeal not just to a segment of the population but to all citizens, operating companies in an ethical and environmentally and socially responsible fashion would become more profitable and therefore much easier to justify.

Acquiring a Powerful Long-Term Shareholder Group

Finally, another advantage corporations gain by donating repurchased shares to the Universal Fund has to do with the nature of the Fund and of citizen-shareholders themselves. Because the Fund does not try to "beat the market" by buying and selling shares, and because citizen-shareholders cannot transfer their interests in their shares but must hold them during their entire lifetimes, the Fund and its citizen-shareholders are indifferent to short-term gyrations in a company's stock price. They are fundamentally long-term, diversified investors. This means that a Universal Fund would create a new and increasingly powerful shareholder group with no incentive to pressure companies to sell assets, take on debt, cut payroll and research and development, or act unethically or illegally to raise share price. To the contrary, they want the companies in the Fund to operate sustainably and to make the long-term investments that lead to long-term financial success. They also want those companies to operate in ways that benefit—not harm—their broader interests as employees, customers, taxpayers, and voters.

Donating shares to the Fund would allow companies to acquire a new kind of shareholder to counterbalance the narrow financial interests that have captured control of so many of our largest firms. It is these narrow interests—many of which don't have a direct economic stake (much less a long-term stake) in the success of the companies they control, and don't have any incentive to take account of the welfare of average Americans—that drive so many corporate directors and managers to operate companies in ways they intuit are not desirable from either a business or moral perspective. Donating repurchased shares makes it easier for corporations to do what so many of their directors and managers want them to do—to operate in a sustainable, socially and environmentally responsible fashion that ultimately benefits all.

Individuals Also Have Strong Motivations to Donate

Perhaps the first question to ask in examining why individuals would donate substantially to the Universal Fund is why do individuals ever donate substantial amounts to any charity? Perhaps you care deeply about the cause? Perhaps you are driven by tax considerations? Or perhaps you are relatively indifferent because you have acquired enough wealth so that spending more on yourself—buying another sports car, another vacation home, another luxury vacation, another yacht—brings little satisfaction. (It's what economists call the principle of declining marginal utility.) And after you've passed on, your money brings you no personal satisfaction at all. You really can't take it with you.

Some of the very wealthy try to solve this problem by building dynasties. But for many and possibly most, the prospect of leaving enormous amounts of unearned wealth to their children (assuming they have any) might seem unattractive. Most parents want to make sure their kids are economically secure. However, most are also likely to be concerned that they do not unwittingly create heirs who are entitled, dissatisfied, dissolute, dysfunctional, and depressed. Perhaps in a perverse twist, studies find that children of the affluent are actually more likely to be depressed, anxious, and at risk for substance abuse.[15] As Warren Buffett explained to *Fortune* magazine, his goal is to leave enough money to his children "that they would feel they could do anything, but not so much that they could do nothing."[16]

Estate taxes also factor into the decision of how much one might leave to one's heirs. Federal estate taxes currently apply to any individual who leaves more than $11,180,000 to heirs. Rates begin at 18 percent and rise quickly to 40 percent. For those above the tax threshold, this greatly increases the attractiveness of making charitable bequests, since many are not thrilled by the idea of leaving nearly half their wealth to the IRS. The end result, as David Callahan puts it in *The Givers*, is that "many wealthy people aren't keen to see much of their fortunes one day going to estate taxes— or, maybe even worse, being passed down to their children." To those with large fortunes (and there are more of them each day), "philanthropy is the only real place the money can go."[17]

If donations to the Universal Fund were made tax deductible, there would be special tax benefits to donating stocks.[18] In many cases, the wealthy individuals who would donate to the Fund would have made their wealth by building successful businesses in which they retain large amounts of stock that is now worth far more than they paid for it. If legislation making donations to the Fund tax-deductible were passed, the donor could get money now in the form of tax savings, in return for a donation of securities that, if the donor were to sell them instead, would trigger a substantial capital gains tax bill.[19]

The bottom line is that, if donations to the Universal Fund were made tax deductible and excluded from estate taxes, individuals would reap substantial financial benefits from donating to the Universal Fund. These would be in addition to the nonfinancial benefits we are about to explore.

Nonfinancial Benefits

Charitable giving is part of many cultures. For example, the concept of tithing (routinely donating a part of your income or wealth, often one-third or 10 percent, to a religious or other social welfare institution) is seen in Mesopotamian, Jewish, Sikh, Muslim, and many Christian religious traditions, including those of the Church of Jesus Christ of Latter-Day Saints (Mormons). But philanthropy is especially prominent in American culture. The National Philanthropic Trust reports that in 2016, Americans donated nearly $400 billion to charity. Approximately sixty-three million of them—25 percent of the adult population—also volunteered their time. High-net-worth households are particularly willing to be generous; more than 90 percent give to charity.[20] In August 2010, Warren Buffett, along with Bill and Melinda Gates, organized the Giving Pledge, an open invitation for billionaires to publicly commit to donating half or more of their wealth to philanthropy. So far, the Giving Pledge has been signed by 184 of the world's richest individuals, couples, and families.[21]

Why do so many people give so much? As many studies in economics, psychology, and neuroscience have shown, and as a number of self-help books will tell you, giving to and helping others makes people happier.[22] Americans in particular have taken this lesson to heart, and consistent with their optimism and belief in the future, they often give because they hope to change the world and make it better. This may be especially true for the ultrawealthy, who often enjoy a sense of what has been called "hyperagency"—the belief that their actions can actually make a difference.[23] Citizen Capitalism addresses such a wide range of issues that are widely perceived to be problems, and is consistent with and indeed promotes so many widely embraced American values, that it is likely to appeal to a large portion of those who want to use their charitable dollars to make our nation a stronger nation and the world a better place.

A second attractive aspect of donating to the Universal Fund is that it greatly simplifies the task of deciding who or what to donate to. Would-be donors today are confronted with a bewildering array of organizations and initiatives to which they could lend their support. There are over a million nonprofits registered in the United States, and more are appearing every day. Moreover, even after deciding which social problem is of particular interest to them—a task that itself is so difficult many high-net-worth donors hire consultants to help them[24]—there remains the job of gauging the organization's effectiveness. Many nonprofits have high overhead costs, which is unappealing to donors who may have made their fortunes through close attention to the bottom line in a business. Some donors with a personal vision prefer to create their own foundations. But foundations, too, often have high administrative costs. In contrast, the administrative costs associated with the Universal Fund would be minimal, and the range of social and economic problems it addresses is wide enough to capture many of the issues donors are likely to care most about.

Ultrawealthy individuals may also be especially inclined to donate to the Universal Fund because many perhaps recognize, and are grateful for, the opportunities and advantages they enjoy that may not be available to everyone else. Not everyone can enroll in an elite private university, or hire a top lawyer to win a legal dispute, or consult a prominent medical expert about a worrisome condition, or even put a healthy meal on the table every night. Many of the ultrawealthy have at least an intuitive sense that they receive more than their fair share of the benefits from our common legacy of natural resources, infrastructure, civic institutions, and culture and want to extend similar opportunities to others. By promoting a more egalitarian distribution of influence and income, Citizen Capitalism appeals to this sense of fairness. It's no coincidence that Facebook cofounder Chris Hughes named his book proposing a UBI *Fair Shot*.

And Citizen Capitalism serves another fairness concern, one shared by wealthy and nonwealthy alike: concern for fairness to future generations. Most responsible people care not only about their own welfare but also about their children, grandchildren, and the generations who will follow us. But future generations have no dollars to spend in the market, no votes to secure politicians' attention, and no shares to vote in corporate director elections. Their interests are ignored by our market, political, and corporate systems, as are the interests of nature and the environment. By creating a new empowered class of long-term citizen-shareholders indifferent to share prices and attentive to corporations' long-term economic, social, and environmental performance, a Universal Fund could help us all be better stewards of the nation and the planet. They can repay the "primordial debt" they owe for the natural resources past generations have preserved and the knowledge, infrastructure, institutions, and culture they have bequeathed to them by paying it forward through Citizen Capitalism.

In the process, the individuals and corporations who donate to the Universal Fund will also create for themselves an enduring legacy. No one wants to be forgotten. The names of the pioneering donors who make Citizen Capitalism a reality will be remembered for a long, long time.

In the coming chapters we drill down on other related benefits of Citizen Capitalism—how it helps drive corporate sustainability; how it gives a diverse range of citizens a voice in corporate boardrooms; how it offers a workable model for renewing support for capitalism; how it fits with broader American values; and how it compares to other similar proposals. We will also discuss possible critiques and challenges.

Chapter 5

How Citizen Capitalism Unleashes Corporations' Positive Power

ALTHOUGH THE UNIVERSAL FUND will be a long-term committed shareholder by design, it is important to ensure that citizen-shareholders decide how the shares in the Fund are voted. Proxy services will provide that function.

Under our plan, citizen-shareholders would be able to select which qualified proxy advisory service best represents their interest as everyday citizens and shareholders, and the Fund would pay for the costs of using the proxy service. This is an important set of conditions, which does two things. First, it eliminates cost as a consideration, which would presumably lead citizen-shareholders to select proxy services that represent their interests, and second, it incentivizes the development of alternative proxy advisory firms with a long-term value focus. As we saw, current proxy advisory services cater to institutional investors. Making proxy advisory services available to each individual citizen-shareholder allows a diverse range of citizens a say in corporate elections.

Through the use of qualified proxy advisors, the Fund would offer a means for citizen-shareholders to vote in a collective and informed manner that would counter many of the distortions in today's corporate governance system. The Fund would truly be a long-term shareholder, and the long-term investment commitment of the Fund will likely be reflected in the voting preference of citizen-shareholders. In fact, short-term voting strategies would be inconsistent with the long-term commitment of the Fund—remember that Universal Fund administrators do not trade shares in the portfolio, thus voting strategies that would reap benefit from "squeezing" a corporation and walking away would not bear fruit.

The proxy services we envision would feature three important characteristics: (1) they would be paid for by the Universal Fund and not by citizen-shareholders, (2) they would be transparent, and (3) they would be nonprofit.

Citizen-Shareholders' Proxy Services Will Be Paid by the Universal Fund

One of the most important elements of our proposal for Citizen Capitalism is that it allows those who register to receive a citizen-share to select a proxy service that would *be paid for by the Fund.* In other words, citizen-shareholders could decide which proxy service's guidelines determine how their portion of the stocks in the portfolio are voted. But cost is not a consideration in their decisions. This leaves them free to select the proxy service whose guidelines most authentically represent what they really want corporations to do.

This is a critical distinction between the proxy services we envision and today's service. Today's services are for-profit entities that compete for market share by seeking out the largest potential clients and by giving them what they want. Unfortunately, as previously discussed, the largest potential clients are mutual and pension fund managers, who are effectively forced by SEC regulations to vote their shares, and whose culture, education, and incentive structure have not traditionally inculcated a focus on longer-term results, much less nonfinancial concerns. Instead, these potential clients may rationally determine that it is more cost-efficient to outsource the noncore and messy job of voting logistics to proxy advisors, plus in return they receive some regulatory "cover"—after all, there is no safer strategy for keeping regulators off your back than to do what everyone else in your industry is already doing as cheaply as possible. Moreover, some have argued that to the extent fund managers care at all about the substance of the voting guidelines the services develop, they want the guidelines to encourage companies to focus on raising share price as quickly as possible.

The result is that today's proxy services guidelines are often criticized for being fickle, "one size fits all," and quick to embrace corporate governance fads and fashions like stock options or "de-staggering" corporate boards so activists can more easily remove recalcitrant directors. Not surprisingly, empirical studies back-testing whether companies that had followed the proxy services' guidelines in the past in fact performed better than companies that did not concluded it made no difference, even though "performance" was defined narrowly in terms of financial returns to shareholders over short periods of time.[1]

Fund-approved proxy services would also want to seek out the largest possible potential customer base and compete for those customers by giving them what they want. In our case, however, the potential customer base is citizen-shareholders. And, because they do not have to foot the bill, citizen-shareholders would be free to focus entirely on the quality of the proxy services' guidelines and the extent to which they authentically serve citizen-shareholders' interests—not on finding someone to do the job at the lowest possible cost. The proxy services, in turn, would compete with each other to develop guidelines that appeal to citizen-shareholders, including competing to persuade citizen-shareholders that their guidelines are the best informed and the most attuned to citizen-shareholders' interests.

Citizen-Shareholders' Proxy Services Will Be Transparent

All relevant information about the Universal Fund and its portfolio would be public: the contents of and the returns to the portfolio; the identities, backgrounds, and independence of the administrators; all Fund financial records (which should be audited); and all records of donations and disbursements.

Similar transparency would be demanded of any proxy service that wanted to provide voting guidelines to, and vote the shares of, citizen-shareholders. It would have to disclose how its organization was structured; the identities, backgrounds, and possible conflicts of interest of its managers; all its financial information, including balance sheets, earnings statements, and statements of cash flows; how its guidelines were developed; and even the guidelines themselves.

This would increase the information available to the public compared to today's scenario. For example, both ISS and Glass Lewis currently are, and for many years have been, private companies, and private companies disclose relatively little information, financial or otherwise, to the public. Moreover, current guidelines are generally only accessible to paying clients.[2]

Openness and transparency are essential for accountability. Citizen-shareholders would be entitled to shine the brightest of lights on the proxy services that guide their voting.

Citizen-Shareholders' Proxy Services Will Be Nonprofit

Finally, we believe that the Fund should require that any proxy service that wants to serve citizen-shareholders must be organized as a nonprofit enterprise. Entities run on a for-profit basis are subject to pressures to maximize returns that can be inconsistent with delivering the best possible service to clients, especially when (as in the case with the Fund and its citizen-shareholders) the clients are not paying the bill. Indeed, many governance experts believe this is exactly why many projects are pursued through nonprofit organizations in the first place.[3]

Another advantage to a nonprofit structure is that it minimizes the chance that, after a particular proxy service has developed a reputation for providing authentic, high-quality voting guidelines, it might be purchased by special interests seeking to use it to gain influence. For-profit organizations have owners that can stand to gain from "selling out." Nonprofit organizations, in contrast, cannot be bought or sold. They can only be closed down or dissolved, and their assets given to another nonprofit organization.

Finally, nonprofits by their very nature tend to attract managers and employees who are motivated less by the desire for personal advancement and more by the desire to help the nonprofit organization accomplish its mission—in this case, providing voting guidelines that advance the authentic interests of citizen-shareholders.

Reclaiming Your Other Vote— Citizen Capitalism Will Give Average Americans a Powerful, Authentic Voice in the Corporate Sector

Most individuals understand the power of exercising their right to vote in *political* elections. When it comes to voting in corporate elections, however, most individuals do not exercise their right to vote. The opposite is true for institutional investors. More than 85 percent of institutional investors vote their shares, while only approximately 27 percent of individual Americans who own shares directly actually vote.[4] That means that 73 percent of all potential individual votes in corporate elections each year are simply discarded. As we saw, the result is a power vacuum that has been filled by a collection of narrow special interests that include portfolio managers, activist hedge funds, and proxy advisory services. Only one of these three groups—hedge funds—actually has any direct economic interest in any of the shares they vote, and their interest typically is in only a few companies, for only two years or less. None of the three has reason to care about the impacts corporations have on their employees, customers, suppliers, or longer-term shareholders—much less concern for our nation, the environment, the other people who populate the globe, or future generations.

However, share voting is immensely important—with it comes the power to elect and influence directors and shift corporate decision-making. In turn, the decisions that corporations make affect each and every one of us in both obvious and nonobvious ways in our daily lives—some more personal than others, such as compliance with safety standards for the installation of air bags. Others are more "behind the scenes," such as supply chain management, which affects whether your favorite T-shirt was made by a child or in compliance with human rights principles. Yet many of us do not exercise our vote.

The Fund makes it easier for individual citizens to earn a right to vote in corporate elections and to exercise this right to vote in an informed and collective fashion. Rational apathy and free-rider tendencies could be reduced by the availability of free (from the citizen-shareholders' point of view) proxy advisory services. The Universal Fund is designed to incentivize individual shareholders to control their right to vote, and it provides average Americans with a path to exercising voice through share voting.

Providing a path for more democratic participation in corporate elections also has implications for the relationship between business and politics. When our political system listens mostly to business interests and the wealthy, the capture of corporate power translates to the capture of political power as well. Citizen Capitalism offers to democratize both, dramatically increasing the range of voices heard in corporate boardrooms. Guided by transparent, nonprofit proxy services without disabling conflicts of interest, citizen-shareholders can help corporations expand their time horizons and the range of interests they serve.

Of course, this is not to say that *all* citizen-shareholders will choose to exercise their vote in a manner that supports the type of long-term sustainable value that the Universal Fund is intended to engender. One can imagine a citizen-shareholder who would rather go for a quick short-term return than vote in a manner that supports long-term gains. That said, we are both optimistic and pragmatic in how we envision shares being voted. First, we know that investments in the sustainable, responsible-impact category make up approximately 22 percent of the market.[5] Similarly, a study shows that 86 percent of millennials indicate that they care about environmental, social, and governance factors in their investment, and nearly 90 percent of them expressed interest in pursuing sustainable investments as part of their retirement savings strategy.[6] Relatedly, another study estimated that by 2020 global millennials may be worth up to $24 trillion.[7] While these data points are for the market at large and are not an exact measure for the composition or behavior of future citizen-shareholders, they do indicate that there is good reason to believe that a critical mass of citizen-shareholders will be motivated to cast their votes in a manner supportive of sustainability and long-term value. Second, the creation and availability of qualified proxy advisors will go a long way in helping individual citizen-shareholders to cast their vote in a collective and informed manner. And third, as author Lynn Stout explores in her book *Cultivating Conscience: How Good Laws Make Good People*, the evidence from behavioral science and other related fields suggests that people are more "unselfish" and "prosocial" than is generally recognized.[8] Research suggests that under the right conditions, most individuals are motivated to act ethically and look out for the interests of others. The Universal Fund is intended to do just that—create the right conditions to motivate individuals and corporations to act prosocially.

Finally, it is worth pointing out that the type of proxy advisory services we envision are not as far-fetched as they might sound. Although currently absent in the United States, close approximations of the type of nonprofit and/or transparent, sustainably focused proxy advisory services that we envision exist in Canada and Europe.[9]

The focus of our discussion to this point has been on exploring the role of corporations in helping address broader social, economic, and political problems, but that given the historical norm of "shareholder value" and the nature in which shares are often voted, the corporate sector's potential has not been optimized. Thus far it has been a lost opportunity. The Universal Fund provides a vehicle for collective, broad-based, long-term investments. Through the related proxy services that we envision, the Fund offers an effective way for shares to be voted in a manner consistent with the long-term, sustainable focus of the Fund. How shares are voted affects corporate behavior. Share voting is a key leverage point in unlocking our corporate sector's enormous potential to help us solve our most pressing economic, social, and political problems.

In addition to tackling the fatal flaws in today's corporate governance system, Citizen Capitalism also has the benefit of helping to address inequality, and it meshes well with certain key American ideals. One of these ideals is capitalism, which we examine in the next chapter.

Chapter 6

How Citizen Capitalism Embraces Capitalist Principles

IN A CAPITALIST ECONOMIC SYSTEM, private property is the primary means of production, and resources are redistributed primarily through marketplace exchanges. It's worth noting here that "pure" capitalism without government doesn't work: government is needed at least to define and protect property rights and to enforce contracts for exchange. Capitalism is sometimes associated with greed, rapaciousness, and the exploitation of the many by the few. Yet the ideal of capitalism rests on a surprisingly community-oriented foundation. From its earliest days, capitalism has been defended not because it allows a few individuals to become very rich, but because it can provide a broad array of social benefits to almost everyone.

Scottish economist Adam Smith's famous 1776 description of the free market as an "invisible hand" begins and ends by emphasizing how this hand can serve the public:

> *As every individual, therefore, endeavours as much as he can both to employ his capital in the support of domestic industry, and so to direct that industry so that its produce may be of the greatest value, every individual necessarily labours to render the annual revenue of the society as great as he can. He generally, indeed, neither intends to promote*

the public interest, *nor knows how much he is promoting it
... He intends only his own security, ... only his own gain,
and he is in this, as in many other cases, led by an invisible
hand to promote an end that was no part of his intention. ...
By pursuing his own interests he frequently promotes that of
the* society *more effectively than when he really intends to
promote it.* (emphasis added)[1]

Capitalism can indeed serve the public interest. When it
allocates resources to their most productive use, it increases the
quantity and quality of the goods and services we enjoy. Indeed,
it is a mistake to assume that this means pursuing unsustainable growth or material consumption. After basic needs are met,
we might prefer capitalism serve our human desires for leisure,
a clean environment, more social connection, better health, and
a longer life.[2] It rewards and promotes investment and innovation. It gives us freedom to make our own decisions. It encourages and rewards desirable characteristics like industriousness,
responsibility, willingness to take risk, and far-sightedness.

This is why Americans have traditionally embraced capitalism. This was especially true in the second half of the twentieth
century, when the decline and eventual fall of the Soviet Union
offered a stern object lesson in the dangers and dysfunction of
communism. By 1991, editorialist Claudia Rosett had declared
in the *Wall Street Journal* that "the free market has won" and "We
are all capitalists now."[3]

Today, many are not so sure. On the heels of the 2008 financial crisis, a number of high-profile best-selling books have
appeared criticizing capitalism, at least as it is currently prac-
ticed in the United States. Rana Foroohar's *Makers and Takers*
and Thomas Piketty's *Capital in the Twenty-First Century* are
only two well-known examples.[4] We see popular movements
like Occupy Wall Street and influential political candidates like

Bernie Sanders, who does not hesitate to label himself a socialist. Instead of fearing the Soviet Union's fate, many, especially younger Americans, now look with envy at the highly regulated Scandinavian nations. A recent poll of young adults nationwide found that 51 percent do not support capitalism and only 42 percent support it.[5]

What's gone wrong? The reasons for capitalism's declining popularity are not hard to find. Without limitation, the purely self-interested can profit from activities that impose "external costs" on others, or simply take money through fraud, deception, cartelization, destruction of competitors, and criminality.[6] The concentration of money and power produces interests with the ability to buy lobbyists, regulators, politicians, and whole political parties, and to use them to acquire further wealth through government subsidies, preferences, and deregulation.[7] In the wake of the 2008 financial crisis, Congress focused its efforts not on bailing out the borrowers but on bailing out the banks and hedge funds themselves.[8] The celebration of self-interest invites greed and wanton indifference to others' welfare, undermining community and social trust.[9]

Citizen Capitalism is designed to counter these problems. Using the tools of capitalism itself—private property and voluntary contract—it allows all citizens to share in the financial returns from the companies whose shares are held in the portfolio. It is worth noting that "private" property does not mean "individual" property; corporations and partnerships are collectively controlled forms of private property that have proven integral to capitalism's success. This sharing of economic benefits gives us all a stake in the companies that are the engines of our economy.

By democratizing control over these corporations, it also makes it less likely they will seek to profit from anticompetitive behavior, production methods that generate excessive external costs, or lobbying for regulation harmful to public welfare. By creating a new and powerful long-term shareholder, it encourages companies to focus on the kind of investment and innovation that drives economic growth.[10] And it does all this in ways consistent with traditional capitalist virtues, leaving donors free to choose whether they want to contribute and citizen-shareholders free to vote and to use their money as they see fit, and avoiding the kind of work disincentives created by programs available only to those who fall below a certain income level or are unemployed.[11]

Openness and Transparency

Openness and transparency have long been recognized as potent tools for addressing many of the negative externalities created by the capitalist system. A well-designed Universal Fund would support these ideals.

Transparency is essential for accountability in governance systems. As US Supreme Court jurist Louis Brandeis famously observed, "Sunlight is said to be the best of disinfectants."[12] An understanding that honesty, openness, and transparency are desirable in both politics and business is reflected in a host of American legal rules, including the Freedom of Information Act, the Government in the Sunshine Act, the disclosure requirements of the Securities Act of 1933, and the constitutional guarantee of freedom of the press.

Unfortunately, in both politics and business, transparency is sometimes hard to find. This is especially true in the corporate world. Privately held corporations, nonprofits, and in some respects, even large public companies have limited duties to disclose information to the public; in some cases, these duties border on nonexistent. Share ownership can be particularly complex and opaque, with individuals and firms using layer upon layer of subsidiaries and shell organizations to hide their activities. As a result, corporations and similar entities are widely used by the wealthy and influential to hide conflicts of interest, launder money, evade legal rules, influence politicians, and sway public opinion.

In 2016, the issue attracted attention when an anonymous whistleblower working at the Panamanian law firm Mossack Fonseca leaked to journalists the "Panama Papers," more than eleven million documents detailing how wealthy individuals, including prominent politicians, had used more than two hundred thousand corporate entities to pursue a host of unsavory and sometimes flatly illegal activities. But the problem is longstanding and endemic. Decades ago, the sugar industry—which knew of the connection between consuming sugar and heart disease from its own research—supposedly paid researchers to produce a 1967 article concluding that reducing cholesterol and saturated fat was the best dietary intervention to prevent heart disease.[13] The finding influenced the advice US doctors gave patients for half a century.[14] More recently, for-profit colleges have created Students for Academic Choice, an apparently student-led grassroots organization that promotes (wait for it . . .) for-profit colleges.[15]

Corporate secrecy enables and encourages political secrecy. Corporations are in a position to give money and media support to politicians, and many politicians are eager to receive them. Both sides would just as soon no one look too closely. We have laws that are intended to force politicians and regulators to disclose whom they meet with and from whom they accept contributions and support. But the laws are easy to evade and difficult to enforce. Average Americans are aware of this—a 2017 survey by Transparency International reported that where 32 percent believed that "most" or "all" business executives are corrupt, even more (38 percent) believed most members of Congress are corrupt, and 44 percent believe that most of those serving in the office of the president and the White House are involved in corruption.[16]

A well-designed Universal Fund promotes openness and transparency on at least three levels. First, the Fund itself should be transparent. So should the proxy services that provide citizen-shareholders with voting guidelines. In both cases, the individuals charged with administering the organization—the Fund administrators and the managers of the Fund-approved proxy services—should be required to disclose their identities, past histories, economic interests, and potential conflicts. Financial information for both organizations should be available to the public.

Giving citizen-shareholders more influence in corporate governance also would promote openness and transparency in the corporations whose shares are held in the Fund portfolio. We don't need laws to require corporations to disclose their activities; empowered citizen-shareholders can demand this of the boards they elect. Admittedly, corporations that disclose matters like their lobbying efforts, their carbon emissions, or the types of research they fund may suffer a short-term disadvantage relative to competitors that don't. However, it's reasonable to believe those corporations would enjoy an offsetting competitive advantage in the form of the loyalty of citizen-shareholders who are also customers and employees.

Finally, promoting corporate transparency promotes political transparency. It takes two to keep a secret. When companies must disclose their lobbying, campaign contributions, and public relations activities surrounding elections, the activities of politicians and regulators are also brought into the light. Citizen Capitalism can use our business corporations to fight political corruption rather than contribute to it.

Belief and Investment in the Future

The revolutionaries who founded the United States were an optimistic lot. It takes optimism to think you can break free from a world power and create a new nation. That capacity to hope has persisted for centuries. Alexis de Tocqueville observed in the nineteenth century that Americans "have all a lively faith in the perfectibility of man ... They all consider society as a body in a state of improvement."[17] It survived well into the twentieth century, as reflected in Americans' embrace of the pursuit of happiness and the American Dream.

But Americans' belief in a better future is wavering. A recent survey by the Pew Research Center found that nearly two-thirds of respondents believed today's children would grow up to be *worse* off than their parents.[18] This is a shocking loss of faith in the future.

To restore citizens' hope for the future, we need to restore their belief in progress: ongoing improvement in the circumstances of their lives. This means not only access to a wider variety of material goods, but also greater comfort, more leisure, better health, more social connection, and more opportunities for new experiences. Corporations can play, and indeed historically have played, a key role in that sort of progress.

Today, anyone who is willing to pay a small fee can incorporate. This is why, although there are millions of corporations in the United States, many of them have only one or two shareholders and no significant operations. However, if we look at the giant organizations we typically think of as "corporations"— the Amazons, Exxons, Googles, Aetnas, Boeings, and General Electrics—it becomes apparent these organizations specialize in pursuing long-term, large-scale projects. This has been true throughout corporate history. Prior to the fourteenth century, corporations founded universities and built cathedrals. In the seventeenth and eighteenth centuries, companies like the Dutch East India Company and the Hudson's Bay Company opened whole continents for trade. In the eighteenth and nineteenth centuries, corporations built railroads and developed the steel and oil industries. In the twentieth century, corporations built the electrical grid, mass-produced automobiles, and developed the internet. Government supported many of these initiatives, but that does not detract from the critical role corporations played in implementing them. Much of what we think of as progress can be credited to corporations.

Yet corporations' key role in promoting progress by pursuing large-scale, long-term projects is threatened by the way the current system places control over many of our biggest firms in the hands of narrow, short-term interests. These interests relentlessly pressure boards to stop reinvesting and instead cut back on basic research and development in order to "maximize shareholder value." By creating a powerful, diversified, and fundamentally long-term investor with no interest in the gyrations of market prices, and with great interest in how corporations contribute to the overall economy, Citizen Capitalism counters these forces. It would give corporate boards more breathing room to plan for the long term and to make the kinds of investments that lead to the breakthrough innovations of the sort economist Robert Gordon argues drive long-term economic growth.[19] Of course, there's no guarantee that any particular company's investments will necessarily pay off; Google's spin-off Alphabet is developing self-driving cars, but so are Tesla and General Motors. It remains to be seen which one will dominate the market. But as long as the Universal Fund is reasonably diversified, citizen-shareholders are not concerned. Whichever company succeeds, they will share in the gains—and they will get to use the cars.

Citizen Capitalism accordingly supports and reinforces a collective belief and investment in a better future. By turning large corporations away from the mindless pursuit of a higher share price and returning them to their historical mission of inventing, developing, and distributing the innovative new products and services that improve citizens' lives, it promises to help restore a common belief in progress.

Paying the Primordial Debt

Many elements of the Universal Fund we propose are in harmony with the ideal of personal responsibility. Citizen-shareholders shoulder the minimal burden of registering for their citizen-shares and deciding how to spend the income they receive from their shares. Nor is that income guaranteed; the financial and social performance of the companies in the Fund portfolio depends, at least in part, on the wisdom of citizen-shareholders selecting a proxy service to vote the stocks in the Fund portfolio. Depending on how the Fund is set up, citizen-shareholders may also play a role in selecting the administrators who manage the Fund portfolio.

But Citizen Capitalism promotes another important, if easily overlooked, dimension of responsibility. That is our responsibility to acknowledge and repay our debts—including, especially, the enormous debt we owe to past generations.

When you become a citizen of the United States, whether by birth or by naturalization, you are given an enormous gift. This is the gift of a fruitful land with ample water, air, and other natural resources; a body of knowledge painstakingly acquired through the efforts of millions over centuries; an immense infrastructure for travel, communication, and energy; a system of world-renowned universities; a remarkable array of political and civil institutions; and a dynamic and diverse culture. Nobel

Prize–winning economist Herbert Simon has estimated that 80 percent of "the income we enjoy today comes not from the efforts of living individuals or existing corporations, but from this shared inheritance."[20] Whatever contributions individual Americans make to society over the course of their lives, such contributions are unlikely to come close to matching the benefits they receive simply for being lucky enough to be alive in the United States today.

For most people, receiving a gift of such enormity generates a sense of obligation to acknowledge the gift and, if possible, find some way to reciprocate it. Anthropologist David Graeber describes the sense that "we are born with an infinite debt to all those people who made our existence possible" as "primordial debt" and suggests that it can be seen in many cultures, both modern and new.[21] To whom, though, is primordial debt owed? To God or another object of religious devotion (as reflected in some practices of tithing or ritual sacrifice)? To nature or the cosmos? To our parents and immediate ancestors? To the king or the nation-state? This last view, Graeber notes, provides a convenient rationale for imposing and collecting taxes.[22]

Among the individuals, groups, and tangible and intangible entities and institutions that have made the lives of present citizens both possible and reasonably comfortable, past generations of citizens are among the foremost contributors to whom they owe a debt. This raises an obvious question: How can one repay a debt to those who have passed on? The answer is in many ways equally obvious, if imperfect: pay it forward, by making their own contributions to future generations.

The idea that those who are alive today owe responsibilities to future generations is reflected in a wide variety of conversations and cultures. Consider the Iroquois Nation's Seventh Generation Principle that decisions about natural resources should be made with the interests of the next seven generations in mind; or Evangelical environmentalists who emphasize Biblical mandates urging humans to act as stewards tasked with taking care of God's creation; or activist groups fighting climate change like 350.org; or conservative political activists' battle against the rising national debt.

Creating a Universal Fund helps citizens meet their responsibilities to the future. First, the Fund is structured not only to provide benefits to its current citizen-shareholders but to continue to provide benefits to future generations of citizen-shareholders as well. Indeed, because the Fund is a perpetual entity that retains the securities in its portfolio indefinitely and accepts donations from individuals and corporations on an ongoing basis, it can be expected to grow larger and generate even greater benefits over time. Moreover, it will also continue to provide opportunities for future generations to repay their own primordial debt.

Meanwhile, by giving diversified, long-term-oriented citizen-shareholders more influence in the boardroom, Citizen Capitalism can help corporations focus on the kinds of large-scale, long-term projects that generate economic growth and innovations that benefit not only current but future generations. The railroads and electrical systems that General Electric and Union Pacific began building in the late 1800s are still serving Americans today. The electric elevators that Otis Elevator Company spent decades to develop and make safe also made skyscrapers—and modern Manhattan and Chicago—possible.

Finally, Citizen Capitalism provides a vehicle for those who are alive today and who care about those who will follow them to express their altruism and concern, both by donating to the Fund while alive or through bequest and by delegating their voting power to a proxy service that supports corporate action likely to benefit future generations. They can truly "pay it for-ward." And by doing so, they not only reaffirm their own integrity and responsibility but also work to heal divisions between the old and young, and between the past and future.

Citizen Capitalism is rooted in the capitalist ethos of distributing resources primarily through market exchanges, but it does not subscribe to a purely self-interested, profit-driven ethos that has become the reigning norm in the capitalist economy. In many ways, Citizen Capitalism is designed to counter many of the problems associated with capitalism, such as short-termism in financial markets and a profit-at-all-cost ethos. The Fund we envision would be designed in a manner that promotes openness and transparency, offers a means for Americans to invest in a sustainable future, and relatedly, provides a means for everyone to pay it forward. The next chapter explores the connection between Citizen Capitalism and certain American ideals.

Chapter 7

How Citizen Capitalism
Mirrors American Values

ANY STRATEGY TO SHIFT A POLITICAL OR ECONOMIC SYSTEM unavoidably encapsulates certain values. A move toward dictatorship prioritizes control over personal liberty. A shift to freer markets promotes individual independence while arguably devaluing cooperation and community. Programs and proposals that are in harmony with a nation's values are far more likely to enjoy political support and to be implemented than reforms that cut against widely held beliefs.

Citizen Capitalism is not only consistent with, but actively reinforces and promotes, multiple ideals and values that are thought of as being deeply "American." Besides the discussed support for capitalism; openness and transparency; hope for and investment in the future; and acceptance of responsibility, especially the responsibility to acknowledge debts to prior generations, these values include egalitarianism, individual liberty, and civic engagement. Of course, these ideals are not exclusive to the United States. Many other countries and cultures share similar aspirations.

However, these values are deeply rooted in American history, psyche, and culture and are emblematic of America at its best. That said, throughout its history there have been looming gaps between American ideals and the lived reality many Americans experience. Most blatantly, there is a jarring discord between the celebration of individual liberty and the legalized slavery that persisted for nearly a century after the Declaration of Independence was signed. Indeed, what one values may be dependent on one's economic, political, and/or racial vantage point. Today, many of us are increasingly concerned that they are drifting even further from the principles they hold most dear. Inequality is growing and social mobility is declining. There is rising distrust in business and the political system. For many, especially younger Americans, hope for the future seems hard to find.

Unlike many other policy proposals, Citizen Capitalism does not sacrifice one value to support another. For example, adopting some type of guaranteed income plan funded by mandatory taxes would promote greater equality, but at the sacrifice of liberty and responsibility. Rolling back environmental regulations prioritizes individual liberty and the capitalist approach, while putting the future at risk and ignoring our responsibilities to those who come after us.

It isn't just about what Citizen Capitalism does. It's also about how Citizen Capitalism does it.

Egalitarianism

The preamble to the Declaration of Independence famously asserts that "all men are created equal." (For the moment we must forgive the Founding Fathers for thinking only of men, and only white men with property, at that.) The word "equality" can have many meanings. We use it to mean "equal opportunity" or "equal treatment" rather than identical outcomes. Few Americans believe everyone should have exactly the same wealth, health, education, and ability. The idea calls up the dystopian future Kurt Vonnegut envisions in his story "Harrison Bergeron," where the attractive, athletic, and intelligent are handicapped with disfiguring makeup, chains, and noise-emitting headphones to keep the envious less-gifted from feeling badly.[1] Most Americans don't find envy attractive and understand that rewarding merit and hard work inspires the productivity, innovation, and investment that ultimately benefits all. Americans are comfortable with a society in which anyone with talent, discipline, and a willingness to work hard can "rise to the top." Indeed, equality of opportunity is one of the hallmarks of the American Dream.[2]

But as Nobel Prize–winning economist Joseph Stiglitz shows in his 2012 book *The Price of Inequality*, differences in drive and merit alone cannot explain the large and growing gaps we see today between the circumstances and prospects of the best-off and the least well-off Americans.[3] It's hard to win a race when your starting line is further from the finish than other contestants. The undeniable reality is that some citizens are given resources, opportunities, and advantages that others are not, and these differences in where they start can determine where they finish.

Most obviously, differences in the circumstances into which a person is born produce great differences in their ability to develop their own skills and pursue an education. The Horatio Alger story is not pure fiction, but it is much harder to rise to the top if you're starting at the bottom than if you're nearly on top to begin with.[4] The children of the elite typically enjoy better nutrition, more stable and less stressful family environments, better early education, greater ability to pay for schools of their choice, and the luxury of taking unpaid internships rather than working part-time jobs. They have ready access to successful role models and useful social connections.

A more subtle source of inequality lies in the ability of the well-off to claim a much larger share of the enormous benefits bequeathed to current generations by prior generations. The US air travel system was built from the past contributions of multitudes, from the Wright brothers, to the founders of Boeing and Lockheed Martin, to the taxpayers who paid for our airports, air traffic control, and safety regulation systems. Yet relatively speaking, it is perhaps business executives and well-heeled tourists who enjoy a disproportionate share of the benefits. Jeff Bezos is rightly lauded for building a mighty corporation in Amazon. Yet he could never have amassed the enormous personal fortune he enjoys today if he had had to pay to raise and educate Amazon's 500,000-plus employees. All citizens benefit from a stable society and criminal justice system that discourages fraud, theft, and burglary. But the wealthy, who have more to protect, benefit far more.

Finally, the top reaches of American society enjoy a third advantage unavailable to many—the ability to use lobbying, campaign contributions, and media outlets to influence legislators, regulators, and popular opinion in order to change legal rules to favor themselves. Examples are legion. Industrial agribusiness has successfully lobbied the US Congress to subsidize the production of corn-based ethanol.[5] The tobacco industry has used supposed "Smokers' Rights" movements to ward off efforts at tobacco regulation, along with extensive lobbying and funding of dubious research denying the health consequences of smoking.[6] The federal tax code has been twisted to offer special protections for the very wealthy. As multibillionaire Warren Buffett observed in the *New York Times*, there's something wrong with a system that allows him to enjoy a federal tax rate significantly lower than the rate his secretary pays.[7]

Individual Liberty

Americans are devoted to liberty. We see this in the moniker "Home of the Free" and in Founding Father Patrick Henry's famous 1775 declaration, "Give me liberty or give me death."

Citizens of New Hampshire still echo Henry's passion with their state official motto of "Live Free or Die."

The irony is that, in creating any state power—whether it be the United States, New Hampshire, or a small township—people create a government with power to coerce them. The state's ability to limit personal liberty is inherent in almost every government act, from war, to taxation, to a police officer issuing a loitering or traffic ticket. So it is understandable that many Americans fear government power to limit liberty. They are reluctant to solve problems with regulation, preferring to leave matters up to the workings of markets. This is especially true for those who follow philosophies like libertarianism or free-market economics.

The tension between government action and personal liberty has ensured that for far too many years, debates over social and economic problems like inequality and environmental degradation have been dominated by two warring factions. One side favors government solutions. The other believes the government cure would be worse than the disease, and matters are best left to be solved (if at all) by market forces. The divide between the two perspectives is often bitter and partisan. Many on the political Left assume only government intervention can do the job, and that anyone who claims otherwise is lacking in intelligence, ethics, or both. Meanwhile, many on the political Right view such ideas as socialism at best and thinly veiled dictatorship at worst. In the words of anti-tax activist Grover Norquist, they want to shrink government until it is so small they can "drown it in the bathtub."

The debate between government and market solutions is old, tired, and divisive. Citizen Capitalism offers to cut through the conflict and the noise. This is because Citizen Capitalism relies on an entirely new alternative strategy for solving our biggest social and economic problems: private ordering. It's a strategy that leaves far more room for personal liberty than government solutions do and also one that allows us to solve certain large-scale problems that market solutions are not well-suited to solve, like environmental damage, large-scale infrastructure projects, inequality, and political dysfunction.

Respect for personal liberty is in its DNA. For example, rather than employing taxes or other coercive government measures for funding, Citizen Capitalism relies on the voluntary contributions of individuals and corporations. They are free to donate assets to the Fund or not as they see fit, and in chapter 4 we explain why many are likely to choose to donate. Nor is anyone required to become a citizen-shareholder. It is up to each individual to decide whether they want to accept the burden of registering. Finally, citizen-shareholders are free to decide how they want to use their share income: spend it, invest it, or give it away.

In this fashion, Citizen Capitalism incorporates many of the most desirable elements of both government and markets approaches. It relies on the kind of individual decision-making characteristic of markets, simultaneously making possible coordinated collective action to achieve large group goals. It offers an alternative approach to social and economic problems that can break through the impasse between Right and Left that has so long dogged debates over how to make the United States a better nation.

Personal liberty is a fundamental American ideal, but it would be a mistake to interpret "liberty" to mean irresponsibility. ("I'll do whatever I want, the hell with you.") A willingness to collaborate and associate to solve common problems has been integral to American culture from its earliest days. As Benjamin Franklin supposedly said just before signing the Declaration of Independence: "We must, indeed, all hang together, or most assuredly we shall all hang separately."

Civic Engagement

More than a half century after Franklin spoke, the French diplomat Alexis de Tocqueville, who had traveled extensively in the United States, wrote his famous ethnography *Democracy In America*. In this treatise—which is routinely taught in college classes today—Tocqueville observed:

> *Americans of all ages, all conditions, all minds constantly unite. Not only do they have commercial and industrial associations in which all take part, but they also have a thousand other kinds: religious, moral, grave, futile, very general and very particular, immense and very small; Americans use associations to give fetes, to found seminaries, to build inns, to raise churches, to distribute books, to send missionaries to the antipodes; in this manner they create hospitals, prisons, schools. Finally, if it is a question of bringing to light the truth or developing a sentiment with the support of a great example, they associate. Everywhere that, at the head of a new undertaking, you see the government in France and great lord in England, count on it that you will perceive an association in the United States.*[8]

Some question whether this culture of collaboration and association has declined in recent decades. In 2000, political scientist Robert Putnam published his influential bestseller *Bowling Alone: The Collapse and Revival of American Community*,[9] in which he argued based on evidence of declines in voter turnout, political activism, and membership in community clubs and organizations that Americans were becoming disengaged and detached, threatening a decline in our "social capital." Others have questioned Putnam's conclusions, arguing that civic engagement has merely shifted forms and can now be found in volunteering and online forums.[10]

There is one area of American life, however, in which disengagement, disassociation, and apathy has become the norm: in corporate governance. Chapter 2 showed how shareholder apathy, when combined with other elements of the way shares are currently owned, traded, and voted, produces a bizarre system in which power over many large corporations has been concentrated into the hands of a small group of hedge and mutual fund managers, and mysterious entities called proxy advisors—many of which have little or no long-term economic interest in the shares themselves but stand to profit from pushing companies to pursue short-term strategies that often harm employees, customers, the environment, and long-term investors.

In terms of both intended outcome and design, Citizen Capitalism offers a tool for creating more equal opportunity in economic participation and corporate governance. In terms of outcome, the Universal Fund allows more citizens to participate in the corporate sector. By giving average Americans more equal influence over the corporations that drive the economy, it gives them more equal influence over the political system as well. In terms of design, the Universal Fund is structured to support the ideal that citizens should be treated equally. This is why, for example, it bars citizen-shareholders from buying, selling, or bequeathing citizen-shares. Just as no voter gets more than one vote, no citizen-shareholder can hold more than one citizen-share. This is also why, in contrast to many recent proposals for a guaranteed basic income, we do not recommend "means testing" and distributing citizen-shares only to those who fall below certain income or wealth thresholds. Every US citizen age eighteen or older can register and receive a share. Of course, especially just after the Fund is created, when the income from shares may be modest, some might prefer not to take the time and trouble to register. That's fine; it increases the benefits to other citizen-shareholders. But by being available to all American adults, Citizen Capitalism embraces the ideal of equality.

By creating a new, powerful, and fundamentally long-term shareholder—the Universal Fund—and empowering its citizen-shareholders to decide how shares in the Fund should be voted, Citizen Capitalism would counter the forces that currently drive companies to destructively chase short-term profits. By distributing shares to all American adults, it allows a far wider range of interests to be represented in corporate boardrooms. And by allowing citizen-shareholders to select a proxy service to vote their shares, it facilitates their task to participate in the corporate sector.

This approach not only promotes civic engagement in corporate governance, it fosters civic engagement more broadly.

Chapter 8

How Citizen Capitalism
Promotes Equality

RISING INEQUALITY OF INCOME, WEALTH, AND OPPORTUNITY
is now widely recognized as one of the most critical problems faced in the United States today. This concern is reflected in recent bestsellers like Thomas Piketty's *Capital in the Twenty-First Century*, Joseph Stiglitz's *The Price of Inequality*, and Chris Hughes' *Fair Shot: Rethinking Inequality and How We Earn* (among others).[1] It has been analyzed in magazines ranging from *The Economist* to *The Atlantic* to *Rolling Stone*.[2] It has become the subject of innumerable newspaper stories, online articles, blog posts, videos, and podcasts.

By many measures, the facts have grown alarming. The income reaped by top earners grows while the wages of the working class stagnate; the top 1 percent now take in nearly 24 percent of all income.[3] This figure has risen from 20 percent in 2013 and is nearly twice as high as in the 1990s.[4] Wealth inequality is more extreme. The top 1 percent owns 37 percent of total household wealth.[5] The top .01 percent (the richest one-tenth of 1 percent) hold 22 percent, a figure that has more than tripled from 7 percent in the late 1970s.[6] Socioeconomic mobility is declining; between 1981 and 2008, the probability of an American moving significantly higher or lower in the earnings distribution during their working career declined significantly.[7]

Not surprisingly, differences in wealth are reflected in differences in stock ownership; although nearly half of all American households have an interest in the stock market, the top decile hold more than 90 percent of all shares.[8] Oxfam International estimates that the wealth of the eight richest individuals in the world, six of whom are American, now equals the wealth of the bottom half of the entire global population.[9]

There are several particularly disturbing aspects to today's economic inequality. First, it is becoming ingrained. Seventy percent of Americans born into the bottom quintile (bottom 20 percent) of family income never make it to the middle class; 43 percent stay stuck in the bottom 20 percent, and the other 27 percent never make it past the bottom 40 percent.[10] The trend is worsening. Between 1981 and 2008, the chances that someone starting in the bottom 10 percent could move into the middle quintile declined by 16 percent, and the chance that someone starting in the middle could reach one of the top two quintiles declined by 20 percent.[11] Americans are starting to recognize their declining social mobility. A 2014 survey by the Pew Charitable Trusts found that fewer than 25 percent believed it was common to begin poor, work hard, and become wealthy.[12]

A second alarming aspect of extreme inequality is how it puts large numbers of Americans at risk for quickly becoming penniless. The 2014 Pew survey found that more than 90 percent of respondents said financial stability was more important to them than upward mobility.[13] Yet in 2015, more than 40 percent of American households did not have enough liquid savings to cover an unexpected $2,000 expense. A car accident, a child's illness, a partner's temporary job loss—any one of these common life events would tip a family into destitution.[14]

A third disturbing aspect is the growing differences in life expectancy based on one's level of income and wealth. A study in the *Journal of the American Medical Association* found that from 2001 to 2014, the life expectancy of those in the top 5 percent of pretax income rose by nearly three years, while the life expectancy of those in the bottom 5 percent increased less than three months. The richest 1 percent of American men now can expect to live fifteen years longer than the poorest.[15] Not only do those at the top of the economic ladder live much longer than those at the bottom, but life expectancy at the bottom may actually *be shortening*.[16] According to the Centers for Disease Control and Prevention (CDC), in 2017 the average American's life expectancy declined—for the second year in a row.[17]

Finally, a fourth, especially ugly element of today's wealth and income inequality is the way it tracks and reinforces the racial, gender, and age divides. Blacks earn an average of 42 cents for every dollar that whites earn, with a net worth equal to only 15 percent of whites. This puts many black households at severe risk of financial crisis. Where the average white family has enough liquid savings to cover thirty-one days of income, the typical black family can only cover five days.

Single women with children are even more exposed. From 1983 to 2013, when the median wealth of single males almost doubled, the median wealth of single women with children fell by a shocking *93 percent*. By 2013, it had fallen to only $500. Although it's natural to expect younger households to earn less and have less wealth than older, more established ones, comparative studies find that younger generations are behind where baby boomers were at an equivalent age when it comes to financial security.[18] Such demographic differences in wealth, income, and economic security divide, alienate, and even enrage many people and undermine American ideals of equal opportunity, cooperative civic engagement, belief in the future, and support for capitalism.

Extreme Inequality Harms All

Although it's easy to see how extreme inequality harms those with the least financial resources, the damage isn't confined. Some degree of inequality is desirable in a capitalist economy. It motivates people to seek employment, work hard, and invest in their own "human capital" by pursuing formal education or acquiring useful job skills. But extreme poverty and insecurity makes this nearly impossible. It is hard to think about, much less to invest in, the future when you're scrambling to meet immediate needs.

Further harm comes from the erosion of the middle class that drives consumer demand. If we define middle class as enjoying an income somewhere between two-thirds and twice the median household income, 61 percent of American adults fit into that category in 1971. By 2015, for the first time in four decades, the percentage of Americans in the middle class fell below 50 percent.[19] The middle class is no longer the majority in America. And, as more and more people have less and less money, domestic demand for goods and services falls.

Most economists agree that because of these two factors— reduced human capital investment and declining demand— extreme inequality harms economic growth. A 2014 study from the Organisation for Economic Co-operation and Development (OECD) found that inequality had a significant negative effect on economic growth rates and estimated that the United States would have enjoyed 20 percent more economic growth from 1990 through 2010 if its income disparities had not widened during that period.[20]

Yet rising economic inequality and insecurity does more than just slow America's economic growth. It also widens social divisions, erodes support for pro-business policies, promotes nationalist political movements, and triggers protests like Occupy Wall

Street's months-long encampment in downtown Manhattan's Zuccotti Park. It incites the kind of hostility captured in the title of Douglas Rushkoff's 2016 book *Throwing Rocks at the Google Bus: How Growth Became the Enemy of Prosperity*.[21]

Writing for the World Economic Forum—the association of the world's elite that gathers annually in Davos, Switzerland—hedge fund manager Alberto Gallo observed, "The alternative to redistribution is instability and crisis. Inequality provides fertile ground for populist parties to harvest support... Over time, populist policies can destabilize democracies, turning them toward nationalism, militarism, and anti-capitalism. The outcome of populist regimes in history ranges from higher taxes, to nationalizations and violations of private property, to commercial and military conflicts ... The cost of sharing opportunity and wealth may be high for today's elites, but the alternative is far worse."[22] Increasingly, the very rich speak of pitchforks and guillotines.[23]

What's Driving Increasing Inequality?

As bad as the situation is, there's reason to believe that without action it will get worse. Few would argue today that increasing inequality is mostly the result of working and middle-class Americans suddenly becoming more lazy and shortsighted. Structural factors drive the trends. Let us consider three in particular: automation, differences between returns to capital and returns to labor, and the connection between wealth and influence.

Automation

Between 2000 and 2016, the US lost five million factory jobs; one study found nearly 90 percent were lost to automation.[24] A recent report from consulting company McKinsey estimated that by 2030, automation could destroy as many as seventy-three million more US jobs.[25] Nor will the losses be confined to blue-collar work. With the development of artificial intelligence, many experts believe automation will reduce the need for human expertise in a range of professions. Computers and algorithms will replace teachers, doctors, lawyers, accountants, architects, financial advisers, even artists and musicians. Historian and futurist Yuval Noah Harari has predicted the creation of a "global useless class," i.e., as artificial intelligence gets smarter and more widespread, more and more humans will find their careers displaced.[26]

Massive job losses would not be a definitive problem if all these newly unemployed Americans had other ways of paying the rent and putting groceries on the table. John Maynard Keynes dreamed of a future in which productivity increases solved what he called "the economic problem" of providing goods and services, and people were able to enjoy a higher standard of living while working only fifteen hours a week.[27] Keynes feared the biggest challenge would be boredom.

Returns to Capital vs. Returns to Labor

Keynes also assumed that in the future, productive capital—including the robots, algorithms, computers, and other valuable machines that are going to produce the goods and services people once did—would be so evenly distributed among the population that all could fund their leisure with its returns. Things have not worked out that way. Because wealth is highly concentrated, the ownership of productive capital is highly concentrated. Because the ownership of productive capital is highly concentrated, the income from productive capital is concentrated. So, it is the owners of productive capital, whether physical, financial, or intellectual, and not the owners of increasingly irrelevant "human" capital, who will reap the benefits of increasing productivity. They will continue to become richer and richer, while those who sell their labor to make a living become poorer.[28]

This thesis is explored in 600-plus pages in Thomas Piketty's 2014 *Capital in the Twenty-First Century*, a weighty academic tome that reached the number one spot on Amazon's bestseller list and sold out at major bookstores. Piketty clearly hit a nerve, and his success inspired critiques. But his basic point—without interventions, structural forces will ensure wealth becomes more and more concentrated in the hands of the rich—is hard to dismiss.

Piketty's own favored intervention is a wealth tax, i.e., a tax on the market value of all assets owned, such as real estate, bank deposits, and assets in an insurance plan. This is typical of would-be reformers who want to address rising inequality: they look to government-imposed redistribution. The type of redistribution plan can differ. It might be a wealth tax, or a more progressive income tax, or an earned income tax credit, or a universal basic income (UBI) program. The problem with all these approaches, however, is that they run head-on into the third structural reason why inequality seems likely to increase. That third reason is that the rich can use their wealth to buy political power and influence, which they can then use to protect their wealth and to acquire even more wealth.

Political Power and Influence

In 2012, Princeton political science professor Martin Gilens published *Affluence and Influence: Economic Inequality and Political Power in America*. Gilens had studied nearly two thousand proposed policy changes and the degree of support each enjoyed among poor, middle-class, and affluent Americans (defined as those in the top earning decile, earning more than about $145,000 annually). He found that when a policy was supported only by poor and middle-class Americans, the statistical like-lihood of the policy being implemented was *near zero*. In con-trast, when a policy was supported by the top 10 percent, it was adopted 45 percent of the time.[29] A 2014 article that Gilens coau-thored with Northwestern professor Benjamin Page found sim-ilar results. Gilens and Page concluded that while business interests and the affluent had influence, "the preferences of aver-age Americans appeared to have only a minuscule, near-zero, statistically non-significant impact on public policy."[30]

These results should not be surprising. Recent history offers innumerable examples of laws and regulations benefiting wealthy interests that had been embraced by Congress, federal regulators, and even the courts, and equally many examples of policies that would have burdened the wealthy that have failed. Joseph Stiglitz catalogs several in a 2015 report he prepared for the Roosevelt Institute, *Rewriting the Rules of the American Econ-omy: An Agenda for Growth and Shared Prosperity.* They include: subsidies for "too big to fail" banks in the wake of the financial crisis; repeated failures to reimplement a financial transaction tax on stock, bond, and derivative trading by Wall Street firms; strengthened intellectual property rights for large corporations; reduced top marginal income tax rates for the wealthy; raised barriers to unionization; weakened labor standards; repeated refusals to adopt guaranteed pre-K childcare; and reduced ben-efits from social welfare programs like food stamps, Aid to Fami-lies with Dependent Children, and Medicaid. Stiglitz could have added many more, including judicial opinions granting corpora-tions constitutional rights, and changes in the bankruptcy code to make it tougher for students and credit card holders to seek protection in bankruptcy court but easier for derivatives trad-ers to do so. In his entertaining but depressing 2010 book *Grift-opia*, Matt Tiabbi describes in detail how the Troubled Asset

Relief Program (TARP) implemented to stabilize markets after the 2008 financial crisis ended up enriching Wall Street bankers and hedge funds. Jesse Eisinger's recent bestseller *The Chicken-shit Club* shows how the wealthy can use their wealth to insulate themselves even from criminal prosecution.[31] Our point is that, if even a minority of the wealthy—including, importantly, wealthy corporate interests—favor a law or regulation, that law or regulation becomes significantly more likely to be adopted. The process works, equally or more powerfully, in reverse. If a significant number of wealthy and powerful interests oppose a policy change, whether for philosophical reasons or out of sheer self-interest, it might be debated, but it won't be implemented.

Citizen Capitalism as a Path Forward

Through the Universal Fund, Citizen Capitalism offers a potential intervention in the following ways.

First, in terms of income inequality, any citizen eighteen years or older is eligible to become a citizen-shareholder, and all citizen-shareholders will have a right to an equal share in income from the Fund. Of course, if both ultrawealthy and low-income individuals become citizen-shareholders because they will each get the same amount of supplemental income, there is an argument to be made that receiving income from the Fund will *not* ameliorate the income gap. Thus assuming A has an annual income of $10,000 and B has an annual income of $1,000,000, if A and B both sign up to become citizen-shareholders they both will get the same amount of supplemental income. So if the Fund paid $1,000, A's income would become $11,000 and B's income would become $1,001,000, but the gap between A and B's income would be exactly the same ($990,000) with or without income from the Fund. And this argument is indeed correct. However, it elides the point that unlike a typical mutual fund or most other investment vehicles that usually require some minimum deposit, access to participation in the Fund is not dependent on wealth or income; it is open to all. The Fund is quintessentially a paradigm of equal opportunity.

Second, in terms of wealth inequality, the Fund provides a free on-ramp to wealth creation to interested citizen-shareholders. Wealth usually takes a longer amount of time to acquire than income, and one's ability to acquire and amass wealth is closely linked to a range of socioeconomic factors, such as a person's level of education, whether one has the good fortune of being a recipient of an inheritance or the named beneficiary to a trust fund, and one's social status and ability to access and leverage networks. As such, the ability to acquire wealth is highly dependent on a number of factors and is not the same for everyone. If only reality was like a game of Monopoly where each player starts with the same amount of cash and at the start of the game each has an equal opportunity to buy property and amass wealth. Yet we all know that this is not the case. The Universal Fund offers a means to equalize the playing field. In a way it's like passing "Go" in Monopoly, where barring some contrary instruction, as each player passes "Go," no matter what has happened before, they get $200 that they are free to spend in any way they choose. When the Fund distributes income, a citizen-shareholder could decide to reinvest it in another investment vehicle, or put it toward a deposit on a house, or perhaps use this income to start a business. Any of these actions would potentially be wealth creating, and for some segment of Americans, having a supplemental income could be the difference between pursuing these wealth-creating activities versus not at all. In addition, we can also imagine a financial literacy component being built into the Universal Fund that would be available to all citizen-shareholders interested in learning about basic financial and investing concepts.

Third, in terms of differences in stock ownership, Citizen Capitalism promotes equality of opportunity in capital market participation. Capital market participation is currently skewed in terms of socioeconomic standing. It is estimated that barely one-third of households in the bottom 50 percent of income own stock.[32] Similarly, according to a 2016 Pew report, lower-income households do not have "extra" money to invest in the market, and at the same time, more than one-third of workers do not have access to a 401(k) or other employer-sponsored retirement plan.[33]

A fourth and related point is how Citizen Capitalism avoids reinforcing racial and gender divides in income and wealth inequality. As a quick point of reference, when broken down by race/ethnicity, Hispanics fare the worst—54.9 percent of Hispanic workers do *not* have access to any type of workplace retirement plan. The Fund is designed to allow all US citizens eighteen years or older to become citizen-shareholders at no cost to them. In addition, the application process for becoming a citizen-shareholder could (and should) be designed in a manner that is accessible, with low barriers to entry. Designing the Universal Fund in this manner would ensure the broadest possible participation while equalizing the playing field for participating in capital markets.

Fifth, in terms of the connection between inequality and how it puts large numbers of Americans at risk, having a supplemental income from the Fund could be a lifesaver (in some cases, perhaps literally). An extra $300 or $1,000 might be the difference between being able to buy back-to-school supplies, or being able to pay for that additional medical test for which there is a deductible, or perhaps being able to make ends meet after one's unemployment benefits have run out.

Sixth, the Universal Fund responds in part to the structural chasm between returns to capital and returns to labor. Under our current system, productive capital is highly concentrated, and the returns from such capital are highly concentrated as well. The Universal Fund provides a mechanism for all eligible individuals to share in the returns on capital. This would be particularly important for individuals who currently are unable to participate in capital markets due to lack of access or lack of funds to invest.

Seventh, the Universal Fund offers an interesting experiment in how to construct a community of influence. On one hand, Citizen Capitalism empowers those less well-off, giving them a greater sense of agency and access to returns on capital, and potentially reducing alienation from the broader society. On the other hand, all eligible citizens are able to participate. No distinction is made in terms of income, wealth, gender, geographic location, or any other characteristics. Funded by corporate and individual donations, it has the potential to bridge class divisions, as well as reinforce a sense of community and common interest, together with civic engagement. Moreover, employing private ordering rather than government action or market forces, it goes beyond the stale, bitter debate between Right and Left.

To be clear, the claim here is not that Citizen Capitalism and the Universal Fund offer a magical elixir that can cure all societal ills and inequality as it manifests in its various forms. Rather, we believe that the Universal Fund offers a path forward that incentivizes everyday citizens to become engaged in the corporate sector, that incentivizes the corporate sector to act in the best interests of all stakeholders, and that uses the power of private collaboration to address rather than exacerbate inequality across a variety of dimensions.

Chapter 9

How Citizen Capitalism Compares to Other Proposals

W ITHOUT SOME INTERVENTION, the gap between the best- and the worst-off Americans is only likely to widen. The Universal Fund offers a private intervention without the need for government funding. In fact, government-initiated redistribution is highly unlikely, possibly politically impossible. In illustration, let us take a look at some recent redistribution proposals that have attracted popular attention.

Universal Basic Income (UBI) Proposals

Widespread concern over the growing gap between rich and poor has triggered a flood of books, magazine and newspaper articles, and blog posts on the subject. Many offer specific proposals to address the problem. One policy response to rising inequality that has captured the public imagination in recent years is the idea of a Universal Basic Income (UBI). Under the typical UBI proposal, the government would provide every citizen (under some plans, every legal resident) of the United States with a periodic cash payment that they would be free to spend or save as they saw fit. Payments would be made to all, under many plans without regard to health, wealth, income, or employment status. UBI proposals have been offered from the Left (*Raising the Floor: How a Universal Basic Income Can Renew Our Economy and Rebuild the American Dream*, by former union president Andy Stern) and from the Right (*In Our Hands: A Plan to Replace the Welfare State*, by Charles Murray of the American Enterprise Institute), from Silicon Valley billionaires (*Fair Shot: Rethinking Inequality and How We Earn*, by Facebook cofounder Chris Hughes) and from academics (*Basic Income: A Radical Proposal for a Free Society and a Sane Economy*, by Philippe Van Parijs and Yannick Vanderborght).[1]

The idea is not new. Free-market economist Milton Friedman supported a version of the UBI in the early 1960s, when he proposed a "negative income tax" to subsidize the incomes of the very poor and ensure they met certain basic thresholds. But the UBI has gained new traction, with a flood of recent books proposing some version of it appearing from authors both conservative and liberal, with backgrounds ranging from labor union representatives to internet billionaires to research professors.[2] UBI has become something of a darling of the ultrawealthy, gaining the public support of (among others) Facebook founders Mark Zuckerberg and Chris Hughes, Elon Musk of Tesla and SpaceX, and Virgin Group founder Richard Branson.[3] There has even been testing of small UBI pilot programs in locales ranging from Oakland to Kenya.[4]

There are, of course, substantive critiques. One is that the amount of money likely to be provided under any full-scale UBI would be relatively small. Facebook cofounder Chris Hughes' plan, for example, would provide a monthly cash stipend of $500 ($6,000 annually). This falls well below the official 2018 federal poverty level of $12,140 for a single-person household. But, as UBI proponents are quick to point out, even small amounts of money make an enormous difference to the very poor. It can be the difference between paying this month's rent and being evicted; between buying blood pressure medication or suffering a heart attack or stroke; between taking a taxi or missing a promising interview for a much-needed job.

A second potential problem is that a UBI might create disincentives for work. Given the relatively modest amounts involved, it seems likely such disincentives would be small. Moreover, any work disincentive created by a UBI would be much weaker than the disincentives created by social welfare programs available only to the poorly paid or unemployed, like unemployment insurance, Medicaid, or the Supplemental Security Income (SSI) program. Nevertheless, some UBI proponents suggest payments should only be made to those who can prove they are working or pursuing an education.[5]

Another common criticism is that, even if the payment amounts involved are modest, a UBI program could prove extremely expensive. In response, some proponents suggest benefits could be "means tested" and provided only to those who fall below certain wealth or income thresholds. Of course, this would increase disincentives to work and might stigmatize the program and those who receive benefits under it as a kind of welfare for the lazy and unambitious. Other UBI supporters, including Milton Friedman and conservative thought leader Charles Murray, recommended reducing the cost of a UBI by simultaneously eliminating redistribution programs like Social Security, Medicare, and Medicaid. This would certainly reduce the cost, but it runs head-on into the most critical objection to any UBI plan—it would be, quite simply, politically impossible.

Government-funded UBI programs often involve some form of redistribution. The redistribution may be primarily from the top to the bottom, as in the case of Hughes' proposal to provide cash payments only to those earning less than $50,000 annually, paid for by a new tax only on the top 1 percent of earners. Or, the redistribution may be from those on the bottom to those on the top, as in the case of Murray's proposal to fund a UBI for rich and poor alike by cutting programs like Medicaid and Social Security, which disproportionately benefit low-income citizens.[6] Any attempt to implement either would run into resistance from both sides of the political spectrum.

UBI defenders often frankly admit this. Charles Murray says his program "would work if it existed, but today's American politicians will not build it."[7] Economist Robert Frank says "it is a pipe dream to imagine that an income grant large enough to lift an urban family from poverty could win or sustain political support."[8] Andy Stern is an optimist; he simply notes that a UBI "is no political slam-dunk."[9]

So, let us take a moment to look at another, more subtle and perhaps more politically palatable response to inequality: a citizens' dividend.

Citizens' Dividend Proposals

In some ways, proposals for a "citizens' dividend" look a bit like the Universal Fund. Citizens' dividend proposals begin by finding some valuable asset—real estate, an investment portfolio, or perhaps the oil extracted from a series of oil fields—and setting it aside to be held as the common property of all the citizens or residents of a particular geographical area. When the common asset generates income—rents from the land, investment returns from the portfolio, or oil sales from the oil fields—that income is distributed proportionately to all qualified citizens or residents in the form of a proportionate dividend.

The idea of a citizens' dividend fits better with American ideals of egalitarianism and personal liberty than a UBI. In fact, one of the earliest proposals came from Thomas Paine, a prominent figure in the American Revolution and one of America's Founding Fathers. In 1796, Paine proposed "to create a national fund, out of which there shall be paid to every person, when arrived at the age of 21 years, the sum of fifteen pounds sterling . . ." The money would come from a tax on landowners. Nearly two hundred years later, the state of Alaska in 1976 actually adopted a citizens' dividend plan in the form of the Alaska Permanent Fund. Alaska had just secured ownership of the enormous Prudhoe Bay oil field, and part of the revenues from the field were dedicated to the Alaska Permanent Fund. Under the Alaska Permanent Fund's terms, every person who has legally resided in Alaska for at least one year is entitled to an equal annual dividend based on the Alaska Permanent Fund's average financial returns over five years. Thanks to the Alaska Permanent Fund, every resident of Alaska still receives an annual dividend, which began at around $400 per person in the Alaska Permanent Fund's early years and now averages around $1,000–$2,000.[10]

One of the most interesting things about these and other citizens' dividend proposals is that they are typically not justified on the basis of economic growth or political stability. Rather, they are grounded in egalitarian *fairness*. Recall the idea that all citizens have an equal claim to common resources they enjoy for the simple reason that they are lucky enough to be alive today. All citizens have an equal moral claim to America's air, water, and other natural resources; to its infrastructure built with centuries of massive investment; to its extensive body of useful knowledge and information; to its language, culture, and civic institutions. They even have an equal moral claim to its land, which was created by nature and not by any human being, and which is treated as property for the simple reason that someone some time declared it to be theirs.

This is not to deny that some of the wealth any particular individual enjoys today is due to their additional investment of their own time, skill, and effort. As Paine put it, "the earth, in its natural, uncultivated state was, and ever would have continued to be, the common property of the human race . . . It is the value of the improvement only, and not the earth itself, that is in individual property."[11]

Senator Elizabeth Warren channeled the spirit of Thomas Paine in a famous stump speech made during her Senate campaign: "There is nobody in this country who got rich on their own. Nobody. You build a factory out there—good for you. But I want to be clear. You moved your goods to market on roads the rest of us paid for. You hired workers the rest of us paid to educate. You were safe in your factory because of police forces and fire forces that the rest of us paid for. . . . You built a factory and it turned into something terrific, or a great idea. God bless! You can have a hunk of it. But part of the underlying social contract is you take a hunk of that and pay forward for the next kid who comes along."[12]

A citizens' dividend plan recognizes the equal moral claim all citizens have on the portions of their national income that are due not to their individual efforts but to returns on their joint inheritance. As noted, Nobel Prize–winning economist Herbert Simon estimated that portion to be as large as 80 percent. As Paine put it, "[i]t is not charity but a right, not bounty but justice, that I am pleading for."[13]

But Paine's plan was never adopted. In contrast, Republican governor Jay Hammond's proposal for the Alaska Permanent Fund became a reality. What explains the difference?

The answer is: political reality. Paine wanted his plan to be funded by a tax on landowners, in recognition of the value of the portion of the land that they did not create but were nevertheless able to extract wealth from. In eighteenth-century America as today, political opposition from a wealthy minority sufficed to stop even the most intellectually justified policy from becoming law, because the proposal would interfere with their ownership interests in their land. In contrast, the Alaska Permanent Fund was to be funded by revenues from oil fields the state of Alaska had just acquired. No identifiable individual or group of individuals could claim to own the oil revenues.

State-initiated redistribution appears to be politically palatable only when the resources being redistributed don't already belong to someone. This explains why Norway was able to create its $1 trillion-plus sovereign wealth fund with revenues from the newly discovered North Sea oil fields (returns from the fund are reinvested or used to support various Norwegian social programs). It also explains why our plan for the private creation of a Universal Fund through voluntary donations by corporations and individuals is far more likely to become a reality than even the most thoughtful proposal for a government-funded UBI or citizens' dividend.

That is, the Universal Fund is far more likely to become a reality if corporations and individuals have both the ability and the motivation to make substantial donations: both the way and the will. As we demonstrated, they do.

This brings us to the question of why not?

Chapter 10

Why Not?

THOUGH PRACTICAL CHALLENGES EXIST and specific design questions remain to be ironed out, none present an insurmountable barrier to Citizen Capitalism. For example, questions related to the criteria for selecting Fund administrators, or the application process for becoming a citizen-shareholder, or the size that the Fund would need to be in order to get started, would all require further analysis by the pioneer founders. All of these can be eased if there is a collective will to create change.

We will, however, note that the plan that we have offered might present some *psychological* hurdles because it is new, different, and has not been done before. For starters, we recognize that our solution, because it relies on private ordering, may strike some readers as odd since it might be presumed that all policy problems must be solved either through government intervention or by the market. The battle lines between government action and laissez-faire market solutions have long been drawn. One can reflect on the fervor on both sides created by President Franklin Roosevelt's New Deal and the equal fervor created by free-market economist ideals—think Milton Friedman. As we have discussed, Citizen Capitalism avoids these battle lines by providing a third path grounded in private ordering—an alternative that has proven itself superior to government and market solutions for addressing certain social and economic problems. Models of such successful private ordering abound and include organizations like private universities, the Red Cross, and the

Sierra Club—all private organizations created by the voluntary association of individuals, which serve a particular purpose and have amassed significant assets and influence. Ironically, business corporations themselves are also in large part creatures of private ordering. Citizen Capitalism is simply borrowing a page from a well-developed playbook. We are deploying the concept of private ordering and using it as a policy solution to drive change in the corporate system.

Another psychological hurdle to implementing the Universal Fund is a common but empirically erroneous assumption that people are purely selfish actors concerned only with acquiring financial wealth. Thankfully, this assumption has proven not to be the case by several research studies in anthropology, behavioral economics, biology, cognitive psychology, developmental psychology, evolutionary science, neuroscience, and social psychology. In *Cultivating Conscience*, author Lynn Stout systematically analyzes how contemporary law and public policy often assumes that human beings are "selfish," yet, in fact, humans tend to be "prosocial" and "altruistic."[1] The assumption that humans are selfish also flies in the face of millennia of human altruism, not to mention modern-day individual giving and corporate philanthropy. The prosocial nature of most human beings makes likely that the Universal Fund will be funded in part by individual altruism.

In addition, there is perhaps a natural human tendency to assume that any policy solution we have not seen at work before must suffer from some fundamental flaw and therefore cannot work in the future. In a witty little handbook titled *The Rhetoric of Reaction*, Albert Hirschman maps the reactionary rhetoric that people tend to deploy when faced with new ideas and policy solutions.[2] In particular, Hirschman looked at responses to liberal ideas such as the French Revolution and Declaration of the

Rights of Man, universal suffrage, and democracy. In each case, Hirschman noted that reactionary responses often employed three principal arguments. First is the "perversity thesis"—this is where any action to improve some feature of the economic, social, or political landscape was critiqued for resulting in exactly the opposite of what was intended. Second is the "futility thesis," which as the name would suggest captured reactions that predicted that the proposed advancement would produce no effects whatsoever. Last is the "jeopardy thesis," in which the argument is that the cost of the proposed reform is unacceptable and puts the entire system in jeopardy.

We point these out because we can already predict and, in some cases, have already heard reactionary rhetoric that fits neatly into one or more of Hirschman's three camps. Our plan for the Universal Fund is no more futile than capitalism may have been perceived as futile when it was first conceptualized, nor will it result in the opposite of what we intend (which is creating an investing vehicle that increases economic participation and diversity of voice in the corporate ecosystem). We can confidently make these assertions because our six-point plan anticipates and provides a framework for designing the Universal Fund in a manner that should avoid capture or perversion of its intended goals and ensure its continued sustainability and future existence.

Finally, our plan for the Universal Fund does not jeopardize capitalism, nor does it dilute it or convert it into a socialist agenda. Rather, the framework that we have presented paves the way for a path forward in a manner that honors the brilliance of capitalism and harnesses its power as a tool for building a more inclusive and better future.

Conclusion

What Next?

IN HIS BOOK *Zen and the Art of Motorcycle Maintenance*, Robert Pirsig observes that "if a factory is torn down but the rationality which produced it is left standing, then that reality will simply produce another factory. . . . There's so much talk about the system. And so little understanding."[1]

Pirsig's assertion that we must first understand the patterns in a system before attempting to fix the system is spot-on. In this book, we have attempted to do just that.

Understanding the nature of the corporate system and the elements, interrelations, and connections that exist in the system is the key to understanding why we now have an environment in which corporate behavior and social outcomes are often thought of in distinct silos. However, this need not be the case.

All citizens can play a role in incentivizing corporations to unleash their full potential in service of humanity. The key is to design a new component of the system that does at least three things.

First, it should honor and amplify the full value of corporations. Corporations already provide immense value in the form of new innovations, such as the development of lifesaving drugs, social media platforms, and environmentally friendly products; salaries, retirement plans, and health benefits; tax revenue; and returns on capital.

Second, it should promote long-term thinking by creating a countervailing force in corporate governance that encourages long-term value over short-term wins.

Third, it should drive universal corporate engagement. It should provide a means for more diverse and democratic participation in corporate governance, including underrepresented segments of the population, prosocial shareholders, and long-term shareholders. Having a broader mix of who counts as a "shareholder" has significant implications for the assumptions on what shareholders actually "value." Suddenly, "value" may no longer mean merely financial value or short-term gain. Other values such as the quality of the environment, the integrity of our political system, and the prospects for future generations could be expressed through the shareholder franchise.

The Universal Fund sits at the heart of Citizen Capitalism. Here is what it could accomplish:

- In addition to addressing many of the dysfunctions in today's corporate governance system, the Fund will also provide a stream of supplemental income to citizens and promote equality in opportunity to participate in corporate governance (chapters 5 and 8).

- The Fund will be patterned on the model of a mutual fund, except participation in the fund would be available to each US citizen eighteen years or older, at no cost (chapter 3).

- The Fund will assemble a portfolio of stocks in different corporations, acquired through donations by corporations and individuals (chapter 3).

- The Fund will also accept donations of cash, bonds, and other assets (chapter 3). It will convert such assets through some neutral trading rule, like "purchase a proportionate amount of all the stocks in the S&P 500" or "purchase the stocks already held by the portfolio" (chapter 3).

- The Fund will pass on the income received to its citizen-shareholders (chapter 3).

- The Fund will hold stocks in its portfolio indefinitely (chapter 3).

- Citizen-shareholders will not be allowed to buy, sell, or bequeath their citizen-shares (chapter 3).

- Citizen-shares will be held for life and will revert to the Fund when citizen-shareholders die (chapter 3).

- Finally, in order to ensure that citizen-shareholders are able to exercise their vote in a meaningful and informed manner, the Fund-approved proxy advisory services will be made available to citizen-shareholders, and the Fund will pay for the services (chapter 5).

The Universal Fund is undisputedly a big idea, but it is also eminently practical: it deploys the existing tools of capitalism, not government, to give all citizens a direct influence on corporate actions. The Fund will be an institutional investor benefitting not just a small clique of stockholders pushing for mere financial value or short-term gain, but all. The Fund will be a steward shareholder—able to reward those corporations whose decisions and actions did not harm people, communities, and the environment and to support corporate strategies that support long-term value creation.

To receive information on events and join discussions, you can visit CitCap.org.[2]

If you want Citizen Capitalism to happen, you need to take initiative. As citizens, you can get engaged, spread the word, bring your knowledge to the table, and/or be a founding funder.

We have spent our professional lives studying how business corporations can benefit humanity. It is in this vein that we offer our proposal of Citizen Capitalism. But the book does not end here. Its practical impact begins when all citizens start doing their part.

Notes

Preface

1. CitCap.org will be established by Tamara Belinfanti.

Introduction

1. Robert J. Gordon, *The Rise and Fall of American Growth* (Princeton and Oxford: Princeton University Press, 2016).

2. *Louis K. Liggett Co. et al. v. Lee, Comptroller et al.,* 288 U.S. 517 (1933) 548, 567.

3. Leon Walker, "BP, Shell Biofuel Investments Hit Seven-Year Low," *Environmental Leader* (July 9, 2013), https://www.environmentalleader .com/2013/07/bp-shell-biofuel-investments-hit-seven-year-low; Shell recently trumpeted new plans to develop cleaner energy technologies, budgeting $200 million for investment in its New Energies division. See Julia Pyper, "Shell Plans to Boost Clean Energy Sources," Greentech Media (July 11, 2017), https://www.greentechmedia.com /articles/read/shell-boost-clean-energy-spending-1-billion-2020#gs .GlDWZ8M. This figure is less than 6 percent of the company's 2016 profits of $3.5 *billion*—too little and far too late to avoid the enormous future losses our society can expect to see as atmospheric carbon levels continue to rise. See Silvia Amaro, "Shell Posts Earnings of $3.5 Billion in 2016; an 8% Slide from $3.8 Billion in 2015," CNBC (February 2, 2017), https://www.cnbc.com/2017/02/02/shell-posts-earnings-of-35 -billion-in-2016-an-8-slide-from-38-billion-in-2015.html.

4. Jesse Bricker, et al., "Changes in US Family Finances from 2013 to 2016: Evidence from the Survey of Consumer Finances," *Federal Reserve Bulletin* (September 2017), https://www.federalreserve.gov /publications/files/scf17.pdf.

5. Ben Casselman, "The American Middle Class Hasn't Gotten a Raise in 15 Years," FiveThirtyEight (September 22, 2014), https://fivethirtyeight .com/features/the-american-middle-class-hasnt-gotten-a-raise-in -15-years.

6. Alana Semuels, "Poor at 20, Poor for Life," *The Atlantic* (July 14, 2016), https://www.theatlantic.com/business/archive/2016/07/social -mobility-america/491240.

7. Raj Chetty et al., "The Association Between Income and Life Expectancy in the United States, 2001–2014," *Journal of the American Medical Association* 315 (2016): 1750–1776.

8. Tae Kim, "Indefensible: Hedge Fund Tax Loophole Shows 'Swamp' Still Rules Over Washington, D.C.," CNBC (December 21, 2017), https://www.cnbc.com/2017/12/21/indefensible-hedge-fund-tax -loophole-shows-swamp-still-rules-d-c.html.

9. See generally Lynn Stout, *The Shareholder Value Myth: How Putting Shareholders First Harms Investors, Corporations, and the Public* (San Francisco: Berrett-Koehler Publishers, 2012).

10. FRED, "Nonfinancial Corporate Business, Total Assets, Level," Economic Research, Federal Reserve Bank of St. Louis (2018), https://fred.stlouisfed.org/series/TABSNNCB.

11. CitCap.org will be established by Tamara Belinfanti. You can visit the website to receive information on events and join discussions.

Chapter 1

1. The Sierra Club, "About," https://www.sierraclub.org/about.

2. Laura Johannes, "AARP Faces Competition from Conservative Leaning Groups," *Wall Street Journal* (March 30, 2014), https://www.wsj.com /articles/aarp-faces-competition-from-conservative-leaning -groups-1394667995.

3. National Public Media, "2017: A Record-Breaking Year for NPR on the Radio" (January 2018), https://www.nationalpublicmedia.com /news/2017-a-record-breaking-year-for-npr-on-the-radio.

4. Statista, "Number of Visits to Smithsonian Museums and Institutions in the United States from 1970 to 2017 (in Millions)," https://www. statista.com/statistics/258337/total-number-of-visits-to-smithsonian -museums-und-institutions.

5. Community Associations Institute, "Community Associations in the United States," https://www.caionline.org/AboutCommunityAssociations /Pages/StatisticalInformation.aspx.

6. Congressional Budget Office, "The Federal Budget in 2016: An Info-graphic" (February 8, 2017), https://www.cbo.gov/publication/52408.

7. *Fortune*, "Global 500," http://fortune.com/global500/2016.

8. Congressional Budget Office, "Federal Personnel," https://www.cbo.gov/ topics/employment-and-labor-markets/federal-personnel.

9. Walmart, "Company Facts," https://corporate.walmart.com/newsroom /company-facts.

10. Corning's 2016 Form 10-K, https://www.sec.gov/Archives/edgar/data /24741/000002474117000011/q4201610k.htm.

11. Ibid.

12. Corning Incorporated Foundation, "Financial Statements 2016," http:// www.corningfoundation.org/who-we-are/who-we-are -financial.

13. Senator Bernie Sanders, "America's Top 10 Corporate Tax Avoiders," https://www.sanders.senate.gov/top-10-corporate-tax-avoiders.

14. Stephen Leahy, "Hidden Costs of Climate Change," *National Geographic* (September 27, 2017), https://news.nationalgeographic. com/2017/09/climate-change-costs-us-economy-billions-report. Nor can we expect our government to fill the funding gap; the Environmental Protection Agency's entire annual budget has just been cut from $8.2 billion in 2016 to only 5.7 billion in 2018. See Zahra Hirji, Georgina Gustin, and Marianne Lavelle, "Trump Budget Plan Targets Climate Science," *Inside Climate News* (May 24, 2017), https://insideclimatenews.org/news/23052017/budget-donald-trump -scott-pruitt-climate-change-science-funding-epa-usda-nasa.

15. Negin, "Documenting Fossil Fuel Companies' Climate Deception."

16. Stephen Marche, "Is Facebook Making Us Lonely?", *The Atlantic* (May 2012), https://www.theatlantic.com/magazine/archive/2012/05/is -facebook-making-us-lonely/308930.

17. Stout, *The Shareholder Value Myth.*

18. *Burwell v. Hobby Lobby Stores, Inc.,* 134 S. Ct. 2751 at 2771 (2014).

19. Lawrence Fink, "Lawrence D. Fink's 2016 Corporate Governance Letter," *New York Times* (February 2, 2016), https://www.nytimes.com/interactive /2016/02/02/business/dealbook/document-larry-finks-2016 -corporate -governance-letter.html.

20. Lynn Stout, *Cultivating Conscience: How Good Laws Make Good People* (Princeton: Princeton University Press, 2011).

21. Joel Bakan, *The Corporation: The Pathological Pursuit of Profit and Power* (New York: Free Press, 2004).

22. Unilever, "About Unilever," www.unilever.com/about/who-we-are /about-Unilever.

23. Ibid.

24. Hindustan Unilever, "Enhancing Livelihoods Through Project Shakti," https://www.hul.co.in/sustainable-living/case-studies/enhancing -livelihoods-through-project-shakti.html.

25. Ibid.

26. Danone, "Products & Brands," https://www.danone.com/brands.html.

27. Danone, "A Global Leader with a Health-Focused Portfolio in Food and Beverages," https://www.danone.com/about-danone/at-a-glance /danone-data.html. Danone estimates its annual sales figure to be 24.7 billion euros. We applied the USD/euro exchange rate as of the date of publication of 1.16 USD:1 euro.

28. Grameen Creative Lab, "Grameen Danone Foods Ltd.," http://www.grameencreativelab.com/live-examples/grameen-danone -foods-ltd.html.

29. Ibid.

30. Tamara C. Belinfanti, "Contemplating the Gap-Filling Role of Social Intra-preneurship," *Oregon Law Review* 94 (2016): 67 (discussing corporate initiatives that seek to achieve both financial value and social value).

31. FRED, "Nonfinancial Corporate Business."

Chapter 2

1. Editorial Board, "Where Have All the Public Companies Gone?", Bloomberg (April 9, 2018), https://www.bloomberg.com/view/articles/2018-04-09/where-have-all-the-u-s-public-companies-gone.

2. ProxyPulse, "2017 Proxy Season Review" (September 2017), https://www.pwc.com/us/en/governance-insights-center/publications/assets/pwc-proxypulse-2017-proxy-season-review.pdf.

3. Ibid.

4. Jeffrey M. Jones, "U.S. Stock Ownership Down Among All but Older, Higher-Income," Gallup (May 24, 2017), https://news.gallup.com/poll/211052/stock-ownership-down-among-older-hire-income.aspx.

5. Ibid.

6. Ibid.

7. Rebecca Tippet, et al., "Beyond Broke: Why Closing the Racial Wealth Gap Is a Priority for National Economic Security," Center for Global Policy Solutions (May 2014), http://globalpolicysolutions.org/wp-content/uploads/2014/04/Beyond_Broke_FINAL.pdf.

8. Edward N. Wolff, *A Century of Wealth In America* (Cambridge, Massachusetts: Belknap of Harvard University Press, 2017), 103, table 3.7. In 2001, 52 percent of households owned stock directly or indirectly; this figure has varied from 32 percent to 46 percent from 1989 to 2013 (123, table 3.11b). The top 1 percent of wealth holders own 50 percent of all stocks and mutual funds and the next 9 percent own 41 percent, for a total of 91 percent held by the top decile (103, table 3.7).

9. See ProxyPulse, "2017 Proxy Season Review." Increasingly, many firms that do go public are adopting a classified share structure that concentrates a disproportionate amount of voting power in the hands of initial investors. More often than not, these initial investors are also in the upper deciles of wealth and income, and thus the dual class share structure further solidifies the coziness between wealth and corporate governance influence. Examples of companies that recently have gone public with dual class share structures include Google, Zynga, LinkedIn, Groupon, Facebook, and Snapchat. See Andrea Tan and Benjamin Robertson, "Why Investors Are Fretting Over Duel-Class Shares," Bloomberg Businessweek (July 10, 2017), https://www.bloomberg.com/news/articles/2017-07-10/why-investors-are-fretting-over-dual-class-shares-quicktake-q-a.

10. This figure is based on a summary of the 2016 corporate election season published by Broadridge, which analyzed 4,200 annual meetings between January 1 and June 30, 2016. See ProxyPulse, "2016 Proxy Season Review," https://www.broadridge.com/_assets/pdf/broadridge-2016-proxy-season-review.pdf.

11. Ibid.

12. In 1988, the US Department of Labor took the position that voting proxies of shares of stock held in an employee benefit plan was part of

the plan's fiduciary duty. See Employment Retirement Income Security Act of 1974, 29 C.F.R. § 2509.94-2 (2006) (setting forth the Department of Labor's interpretation of ERISA as it relates to the voting of proxies). To satisfy their fiduciary duties, fund managers sought help from proxy advisory firms. However, the watershed moment for the proxy advisory industry came in 2003 when the SEC passed a new rule requiring registered investment companies to disclose their complete voting records on an annual basis. See Disclosure of Proxy Voting Policies Voting Records by Registered Management Investment Companies, Investment Company Act Release No. n25922, 17 C.F.R. 239, 249, 270, 274 (January 31, 2003). For a general overview of the proxy advisory industry, see Tamara C. Belinfanti, "The Proxy Advisory and Corporate Governance Industry: The Case for Increased Oversight and Control," *Stanford Journal of Law, Business, and Finance* 14 (2009): 384.

13. ProxyPulse, "2017 Proxy Season Review."

14. This causes many fund managers to turn to "active investing": the quest to juice portfolio performance by earning trading profits buying and selling stocks. Actively managed funds are especially short-term investors, holding the shares in their portfolios for an average of two years or less. As Paul Bogle, founder of Vanguard Funds, put it, the mutual fund industry has become a "rent-a-stock" industry. See John C. Bogle, "Reflections on the Evolution of Mutual Fund Governance," *Journal of Business & Technology Law* 1 (2006): 47. For a more fulsome discussion of fund manager behavior, see Lynn Stout, *The Shareholder Value Myth: How Putting Shareholders First Harms Investors, Corporations, and the Public* (San Francisco: Berrett-Koehler Publishers, 2012), 66–67.

15. Stout, *The Shareholder Value Myth*. See also Einer Elhauge, "Sacrificing Corporate Profits in the Public Interest," *New York University Law Review* 80 (2005): 733, 776–817, and Usman Hayat, "Shareholder Value Maximization: The World's Dumbest Idea?", CFA Institute (October 23, 2014).

16. Bakan, *The Corporation*; Aspen Institute for Business and Society, "Overcoming Short-Termism: A Call for a More Responsible Approach to Investment" (September 2009), https://www.aspeninstitute.org/sites /default/files/content/docs/pubs/overcome_short_state0909_0.pdf (describing the risks created by a focus on short-term stock price and performance); the Roosevelt Institute, "Financialization Project, Understanding Short-Termism: Questions and Consequences" (2015), http://rooseveltinstityte.org/wp-content/uploads/2015/11 /Understanding -Short-Termism.pdf (concluding that "by pressuring managers to pay out funds instead of investing them, shareholders are simply reducing production and income in the economy as a whole"); and William Lazonick, "Profits Without Prosperity," *Harvard Business Review* (September 2014), 48, 50, https://hbr.org/2014/09/profits-without-prosperity/ar/1 (arguing that incentivizing executives to

maximize shareholder value led to executives undertaking share repurchases, which in turn led to a failure to translate corporate profitability into widespread economic prosperity). One potential counter to short-termist tendencies and outcomes is the rise of ESG (environmental, social, and governance) funds, SRI (socially responsible investments) funds, and impact investors whose investment strategy seeks to take into account both financial and nonfinancial risks. In 2016, a *Wall Street Journal* report estimated that ESG/SRI/impact investments accounted for 22 percent of the market (approximately $8.72 trillion), which represented a 33 percent increase from 2014–2016. See Matthew Kassel, "How Much Do You Know About Ethical Investing?", *Wall Street Journal* (July 6, 2016), https://www.wsj .com/articles/how-much-do-you-know-about-ethical-investing -1499349815.

17. Letter, dated February 23, 1988, from the deputy assistant secretary of the Pension Welfare Benefits Administration to Mr. Helmuth Fandl, chairman of the Retirement Board of Avon Products, Inc. (the "Avon Letter"). The Avon Letter took the position that the fiduciary act of managing employee benefit plan assets included a duty to vote proxies associated with shares owned by the plan. See also US Securities and Exchange Commission, "Proxy Voting: Proxy Voting Responsibilities of Investment Advisers and Availability of Exemptions from the Proxy Rules for Proxy Advisory Firms," *Staff Legal Bulletin*, no. 20 (June 30, 2014), https://www.sec.gov/interps/legal/cfslb20.htm.

18. US Government Accountability Office, "Corporate Shareholder Meetings. Issues Relating to Firms That Advise Institutional Investors on Proxy Voting," *Report to Congressional Requesters* (June 2007), https://www.gao.gov/new.items/d07765.pdf, 13, table 1; Sheryl Cuisia, Adam Rose, and Eugenie Laurian, "Top 15 Things You Should Know About Proxy Advisory Agencies," Boudicca (January 5, 2017), https://boudiccaproxy.com/2017/01/05/top-15-things-you-should -know-about-proxy-advisers.

19. Cuisia, Rose, and Laurian, "Top 15 Things You Should Know About Proxy Advisory Agencies."

20. See David F. Larcker, Allan L. McCall, and Gaizka Ormazabal, "Outsourcing Shareholder Voting to Proxy Advisory Firms," *Journal of Law and Economics* 58 (2015): 173–178 (surveying past research findings and noting that although it is hard to precisely measure the influence, "proxy advisor recommendations have a significant impact on the voting outcomes on various types of shareholder ballot items"); David F. Larcker, Allan L. McCall, and Brian Tayan, "The Influence of Proxy Advisory Firm Voting Recommendations On Say-on-Pay Votes and Executive Compensation Decisions," *Director Notes* (March 2012), https://www.gsb.stanford.edu/sites/gsb/files/publication-pdf /cgri-survey-2012-proxy-voting_0.pdf (finding that proxy advisor recommendations "have a substantial impact on the design of executive

compensation programs"); Jennifer E. Bethel and Stuart L. Gillan, "The Impact of the Institutional and Regulatory Environment on Shareholder Voting," *Financial Management* 31 (2002): 29 (analyzing the impact of ISS recommendations on governance issues); and Belinfanti, "The Proxy Advisory and Corporate Governance Industry" (discussing the perceived influence of ISS's vote recommendations).

21. US Government Accountability Office, "Corporate Shareholder Meetings. Proxy Advisory Firms' Role in Voting and Corporate Governance Practices," *Report to the Chairman, Subcommittee on Economic Policy, Committee on Banking, Housing, and Urban Affairs, U.S. Senate* (November 2016), https://www.gao.gov/assets/690/681051.pdf.

22. "All Locked-Up," *Economist* (August 2, 2007), http://www.economist .com/node/9596328; "How Hedge Funds Are Structured," Hedgefundamentals.org (June 2016), https://www.managedfunds.org /wp-content/uploads/2016/06/06.09.16-How-HFs-are-Structured.pdf.

23. The Alternative Investment Management Association, *Global Report of 2015*, https://www.aima.org/uploads/assets/uploaded/7da17150-817d -4cb2-9deb771b6f3ab69f.pdf.

24. Sullivan & Cromwell LLP, *2016 U.S. Shareholder Activism Review and Analysis* (November 28, 2016), 7, https://www.sullcrom.com/siteFiles /Publications/SC_Publication_2016_U.S._Shareholder_Activism _Review_and_Analysis.pdf.

25. ValueAct held at least some stock in Valeant for ten years.

26. Nathan Vardi, "Hedge Fund ValueAct Capital's Valeant Legacy," *Forbes* (June 6, 2016), https://www.forbes.com/sites/nathanvardi/2016/06/06 /hedge-fund-valueact-capitals-valeant-legacy/#7c09064f203a.

27. Bethany McLean, "The Valeant Meltdown and Wall Street's Major Drug Problem," *Vanity Fair* (June 5, 2016), https://www.vanityfair.com /news/2016/06/the-valeant-meltdown-and-wall-streets-major -drug-problem.

28. Carly Helfand, "Valeant Starts $500M in Salix Cost-Cutting with 250 Layoffs," FiercePharma (April 6, 2015), https://www.fiercepharma.com /m-a/valeant-starts-500m-salix-cost-cutting-250-layoffs; Tracy Staton, "Shionogi Cutting 350 Reps as BioVail Boosts Layoffs," FiercePharma (September 8, 2010), https://www.fiercepharma.com/pharma /shionogi-cutting-350-reps-as-biovail-boosts-layoffs; Tracy Staton, "Valeant to Fire Thousands, Restructure Ops after Bausch Buyout," FiercePharma (July 29, 2013), https://www.fiercepharma.com /m-a /valeant-to-fire-thousands-restructure-ops-after-bausch-buyout; Business Staff, "Buyer of Dendreon Lays Off 77 Seattle Employees" *Seattle Times* (March 2, 2015), https://www.seattletimes.com/business /technology/buyer-of-dendreon-warns-77-seattle-employees-of -layoffs.

29. Andrew Pollack and Sabrina Tavernise, "Valeant's Drug Price Strategy Enriches It, but Infuriates Patients and Lawmakers," *New York Times* (October 4, 2015), https://www.nytimes.com/2015/10/05/business

/valeants-drug-price-strategy-enriches-it-but-infuriates-patients
-and-lawmakers.html?ref=topics.

30. Melody Petersen, "How 4 Drug Companies Rapidly Raised Prices
On Life-Saving Drugs," *Los Angeles Times* (December 21, 2016),
http://www.latimes.com/business/la-fi-senate-drug-price-study
-20161221-story.html.

31. Peter J. Henning, "As Valeant Struggles, Its Tally Sheet of Scandals
Grows," *New York Times* (March 28, 2016), https://www.nytimes.
com/2016/03/29/business/dealbook/as-valeant-struggles-its-tally
-sheet-of-scandals-grows.html.

32. McLean, "The Valeant Meltdown."

33. Ibid.

34. Alexandra Bosanac, "CEO of the Year: Mike Pearson, Valeant,"
Canadian Business (October 19, 2015), https://www.canadianbusiness.
com/leadership/ceo-of-the-year/top-ceo-mike-pearson-valeant.

35. Pollack and Tavernise, "Valeant's Drug Price Strategy Enriches It."

36. Bausch Health, "Institutional Shareholder Services (ISS) Recommends
Allergan Shareholders Call a Special Meeting of Shareholders," Valeant
News Releases 2014 (August 6, 2014), http://ir.valeant.com/news
-releases/2014/06-08-2014.

37. Antione Gara, "Bill Ackman and Valeant Settle Allergan Insider
Trading Lawsuit for $290 Million," *Forbes* (December 30, 2017),
https://www.forbes.com/sites/antoinegara/2017/12/30/bill-ackman
-and-valeant-settle-allergan-insider-trading-lawsuit-for-290-million
/#17b4dd6f1f32.

38. Andrew Pollack, "Drug Goes from $13.50 a Tablet to $750, Overnight,"
New York Times (September 20, 2015), https://www.nytimes.com/2015
/09/21/business/a-huge-overnight-increase-in-a-drugs-price-raises
-protests.html.

39. Wolf Richter, "EpiPen Is Getting Crushed by a $10 Copycat," *Business
Insider* (March 8, 2017), http://www.businessinsider.com/after
-years-of-price-gouging-mylans-epipen-gets-crushed-2017-3.

40. Ibid.

41. Ari I. Weinberg, "How Activist is Your Index Fund?", *Forbes* (April 25,
2012), https://www.forbes.com/sites/ariweinberg/2012/04/25/how
-activist-is-your-index-fund/#5e1ba6bb7d94.

42. Editorial Board, "Where Have All the Public Companies Gone?"

Chapter 3

1. Our concept of the universal citizen-shareholder should not be
confused with the "universal investor" or "universal owner" label
sometimes applied to large institutional investors like pension and
mutual funds, which are so broadly diversified that they are more
concerned with the performance of the economy as a whole than with
the performance of a single company. See generally James P. Hawley

and Andrew T. Williams, *The Rise of Fiduciary Capitalism: How Institutional Investors Can Make Corporate America More Democratic* (Philadelphia: University of Pennsylvania Press, 2000).

2. This would require legislative intervention, and the tax treatment would depend on how the new regulation allowing the deduction were drafted.

3. The Giving Pledge, "A Commitment to Philanthropy," https://givingpledge.org.

4. Ibid.

5. See generally Guido Calabresi and A. Douglas Melamed, "Property Rules, Liability Rules, and Inalienability: One View of the Cathedral," *Harvard Law Review* 85 (1972): 1089.

6. Although some shareholders nearing the end of their life expectancy may be more short-term oriented (for example, preferring that companies adopt overly generous dividend policies), their interests will be counterbalanced by other, more altruistic or well-off shareholders nearing the end of their life expectancy as well as by younger shareholders who prefer that corporations invest optimally for future returns. This dynamic is different from the incentives of today's shareholders, who typically hold shares for two years or less.

7. Where the typical actively managed stock fund charges expenses of 1.34 percent of assets annually, Vanguard, BlackRock, and Schwab offer ETF equity funds that charge annual fees of only 0.05–0.03 percent. See Heather Long, "The Best Cheap Investment Funds," CNN Money (June 2016), http://money.cnn.com/2016/06/06/investing/invest -in-funds -with-low-fees/index.html. Another point of comparison might be with the management fees charged by the actively managed Alaska Permanent Fund, which charges expenses of less than 30 basis points annually. See Peter Barnes, *With Liberty and Dividends for All* (San Francisco: Berrett-Koehler Publishers, 2014), 73.

Chapter 4

1. John J. Havens and Paul G. Schervish, *A Golden Age of Philanthropy Still Beckons: National Wealth Transfer and Potential for Philanthropy Technical Report*, Center on Wealth and Philanthropy, Boston College (May 28, 2014), http://www.bc.edu/content/dam/files/research_sites/cwp/pdf/A %20Golden%20Age%20of%20Philanthropy%20Still%20Bekons.pdf, cited in David Callahan, *The Givers: Wealth, Power, and Philanthropy in a New Gilded Age* (New York: Alfred A. Knopf, 2017), 18, 318.

2. Edward Yardeni, Joe Abbott, and Mali Quintana, *Stock Market Indicators: S&P 500 Buybacks and Dividends*, Yardeni Research Inc. (July 13, 2018), 3, figure 1, https://www.yardeni.com/pub/buybackdiv.pdf.

3. See Census' table on Electorate Profiles: Selected Characteristics of the Citizen, Voting-Age Population; Danielle Kaeble, et al., "Correctional Populations in the United States, 2014," US Department of Justice, Bureau of Justice Statistic, *Bulletin* (December 2015, revised January 21, 2016), https://www.bjs.gov/content/pub/pdf/cpus14.pdf.

4. Sean Ross, "A History of the S&P 500 Dividend Yield," Investopedia (July 16, 2016), https://www.investopedia.com/articles/markets/071616/history-sp-500-dividend-yield.asp. Although dividend yields have fallen a bit in recent years to just over 2 percent, this is because companies are paying back even more money to shareholders in the form of share purchases, which are the economic equivalent of dividends.

5. Barnes, *With Liberty and Dividends for All*, 73–77; Matthew Berman and Random Rearney, *Permanent Fund Dividends and Poverty in Alaska*, Institute of Social and Economic Research, University of Alaska Anchorage (November 2016), http://www.iser.uaa.alaska.edu/Publications/2016_12-PFDandPoverty.pdf.

6. See Vito J. Racanelli, "The U.S. Stock Market Is Now Worth $30 Trillion," *Barron's* (January 18, 2018), https://www.barrons.com/articles/the-u-s-stock-market-is-now-worth-30-trillion-1516285704; SIFMA, *SIFMA Insights: US Fixed Income: Market Structure Primer* (July 12, 2018), https://www.sifma.org/wp-content/uploads/2018/07/SIFMA-Insights-FIMS-Primer_FINAL.pdf; Heather Rupp, "The U.S. Fixed Income Market," Seeking Alpha (August 16, 2016), https://seekingalpha.com/article/4000049-u-s-fixed-income-market (estimating size of US fixed income market to be approximately $39 trillion); "U.S. REIT Industry Equity Market Cap. FTSE Nareit Real Estate Index Historical Market Capitalization, 1972–2017" (estimating size of REIT equity market cap of $1.1 trillion in 2017), https://www.reit.com/data-research/reit-market-data/us-reit-industry-equity-market-cap; and Scott Reyburn, "What's the Global Art Market Really Worth? Depends On Who You Ask," *New York Times* (March 23, 2017), https://www.nytimes.com/2017/03/23/arts/global-art-market.html (estimating size of global art market sales to be around $50 billion in 2017, of which US sales accounted for 40 percent).

7. Yardeni, Abbott, and Quintana, *Stock Market Indicators* (in the first 2018 quarter buybacks amounted to approximately $750 billion).

8. See Richard Dobbs and Werner Rehm, "The Value of Share Buybacks," *McKinsey Quarterly* (August 2005).

9. This would require legislative intervention, and the tax treatment would depend on how the new regulation allowing the deduction was drafted.

10. See, for example, Sara Bernow, Bruce Klempner, and Clarisse Magnin, "From 'Why' to 'Why Not': Sustainable Investing As the New Normal," McKinsey & Company (October 2017), https://www.mckinsey.com/industries/private-equity-and-principal-investors/our-insights/from-why-to-why-not-sustainable-investing-as-the-new-normal (stating that "[m]ore than one-quarter of assets under management globally are now being invested according to the premise that environmental, social, and governance (ESG) factors"). See also US SIF Foundation, *Report on US Sustainable Responsible and Impact Investing Trends*

(2016), https://www.ussif.org/files/SIF_Trends_16_Executive
_Summary(1).pdf ("The demand for sustainable and impact investing
is growing—investors now consider environmental, social and
governance (ESG) factors across $8.72 trillion of professionally
managed assets, a 33 percent increase since 2014.").

11. See Suntae Kim, et al., "Why Companies Are Becoming B
Corporations," *Harvard Business Review* (June 2016), https://hbr.org
/2016/06/why-companies-are-becoming-b-corporations;
King Arthur Flour, *Benefit Corporation Annual Report 2017*,
https://www.kingarthurflour.com/our-story/bcorp-report.html;
see also "100 Best Corporate Citizens 2018," *Corporate Responsibility*
(Summer 2018), http://www.3blassociation.com/files/exV4MF/CR
_Summer%2018_100%20Best_revised.pdf; "See the Numbers—Giving
USA 2017 Infographic," Giving USA (June 12, 2017), https://givingusa.org
/see-the-numbers-giving-usa-2017-infographic/ (noting that giving
from corporations amounted to $18.55 billion in 2016). Corporate
philanthropy can also attract substantial positive attention.

12. Julia Creswell and Michael Corkery, "Wal-Mart and Dick's Raise
Minimum Age for Gun Buyers to 21," *New York Times* (February 28,
2018), https://www.nytimes.com/2018/02/28/business/walmart-and
-dicks-major-gun-retailers-will-tighten-rules-on-guns-they-sell.html.

13. Global Reporting Initiative, "About Sustainability Reporting,"
https://www.globalreporting.org/information/sustainability
-reporting/Pages/default.aspx.

14. Curtis C. Verschoor, "Sustainability Reporting Increases," *Strategic
Finance* (October 1, 2017), http://sfmagazine.com/post-entry/october
-2017-sustainability-reporting-increases.

15. Uniya S. Luther, "The Culture of Affluence: Psychological Costs of
Material Wealth," *Child Development* 74 (2003): 1581.

16. Callahan, *The Givers*, 43.

17. Ibid., 16, 43. See also at 18 (nearly seventy thousand individuals living
in North America have liquid assets of $30 million or more).

18. This would require legislative intervention, and the tax treatment
would depend on how the new regulation allowing the deduction was
drafted.

19. This would require legislative intervention allowing the deduction and
would depend on the details of the new regulation determining the tax
treatment.

20. National Philanthropic Trust, "Charitable Giving Statistics,"
https://www.nptrust.org/philanthropic-resources/charitable-giving
-statistics; See also Vartan Gregorian, "Philanthropy in America,"
Carnegie Reporter (January 8, 2018), https://medium.com/carnegie
-reporter/philanthropy-in-america-3a63879cb75c; Giving USA,
"Giving USA 2017: Total Charitable Donations Rise to New High of
$390.05 Billion" (June 12, 2017), https://givingusa.org/giving-usa-2017
-total-charitable-donations-rise-to-new-high-of-390-05-billion.

21. "The Giving Pledge is an effort to help address society's most pressing problems by inviting the world's wealthiest individuals and families to commit more than half of their wealth to philanthropy or charitable causes either during their lifetime or in their will." The Giving Pledge, "About," https://givingpledge.org/About.aspx.

22. See generally Jenny Santi, *The Giving Way to Happiness: Stories and Science Behind the Transformative Power of Giving* (New York: Jeremy P. Tarcher/Penguin, 2015); Azim Jamal and Harvey McKinnon, *The Power of Giving: How Giving Back Enriches Us All* (New York: Jeremy P. Tarcher/Penguin, 2008); Christian Smith, *The Paradox of Generosity: Giving We Receive, Grasping We Lose* (New York: Oxford University Press, 2014).

23. Callahan, *The Givers*, 40–41.

24. Ibid., 19. In organizing the Giving Pledge, Bill Gates and Warren Buffett quickly learn that "many of America's richest people had yet to figure out what they would ultimately do with their money," 20.

Chapter 5

1. See Stout, *The Shareholder Value Myth*, 70. For a recent overview on the need for reform in how proxy advisors develop guidelines, see James R. Coplan, David F. Larcker, and Brian Tayan, *Proxy Advisory Firms: Empirical Evidence and the Case for Reform*, Manhattan Institute (May 21, 2018), https://www.manhattan-institute.org/sites/default /files/R-JC-0518-v2.pdf (concluding that proxy advisor guidelines lack transparency, that institutional investors are influenced by proxy advisor recommendations, and that corporations are influenced by proxy advisory guidelines). See also Belinfanti, "The Proxy Advisory and Corporate Governance Industry" (discussing the one-size-fits-all nature of proxy advisory guidelines) and Lynn A. Stout, *Why Should ISS Be the Master of the Corporate Governance Universe*, Dow Jones Corporate Governance (January 4, 2006) (highlighting the flaws in current proxy advisory system).

2. See Coplan, Larcker, and Tayan, *Proxy Advisory Firms* (discussing lack of transparency in how proxy advisors develop their voting guidelines).

3. See Henry Hansmann, "The Role of Nonprofit Enterprise," *Yale Law Journal* 89 (1980): 835 (arguing that nonprofits have what Hansmann terms a "nondistribution constraint", i.e., any net earnings must be retained and devoted to the purpose of the enterprise and cannot be distributed to any residual claimants). As Hansmann described, the nondistribution constraint avoids creating an incentive to maximize profits.

4. ProxyPulse, *2018 Proxy Season Preview and 2017 Mini-Season Wrap-Up*, https://www.pwc.com/us/en/governance-insights-center/publications /assets/pwc-broadridge-proxypulse-2018-proxy-season-preview.pdf.

5. See Kassel, "How Much Do You Know About Ethical Investing?"

6. Audrey Choi, "How Younger Investors Could Reshape the World," Morgan Stanley (January 24, 2018), https://www.morganstanley.com /access/why-millennial-investors-are-different.

7. Benjamin Ernst, Daniel Kobler, and Felix Haubler, "Millennials and Wealth Management: Trends and Challenges of Our New Clientele," *Inside, Quarterly Insights from Deloitte* 9 (June 2015): 56, https://www2 .deloitte.com/content/dam/Deloitte/lu/Documents/financial-services /lu-millennials-wealth-management-trends-challenges-new-clientele -0106205.pdf.

8. Stout, *Cultivating Conscience.*

9. For example, SHARE (Shareholder Association for Research and Education) is a nonprofit proxy advisor based in Canada, and Ethos is a Swiss proxy advisory service focused on socially responsible investments. See SHARE, https://share.ca/, and Ethos, https://www.ethosfund.ch/en/products-and-services/proxy-voting -service. It is worth noting that two of the authors are in the process of developing a nonprofit that would fill the existing gap in the US market. For more information on this nonprofit, see ethicalshareholder.org.

Chapter 6

1. Adam Smith, *An Enquiry into the Nature and Causes of the Wealth of Nations*, Book IV, Chapter II (Edinburgh: Adam and Charles Black; and London: Longman, Brown, Green and Longman, 1850, originally published in 1776) 199.

2. John de Graaf, David Wann, and Thomas H. Naylor, *Affluenza: How Overconsumption Is Killing Us—and How to Fight Back* (San Francisco: Berrett-Koehler Publishers, Inc., 2014); David Pilling, *The Growth Delusion: Wealth, Poverty, and the Well-Being of Nations* (New York: Tim Duggan Books, 2018).

3. Claudia Rosett, "Free Market Victory? Yalta Looms," *Wall Street Journal* (November 8, 1991), A14.

4. Rana Foroohar, *Makers and Takers: The Rise of Finance and the Fall of American Business* (New York: Crown Business, 2016); Joseph E. Stiglitz, *The Price of Inequality: How Today's Divided Society Endangers Our Future* (New York London: W. W. Norton & Company, 2012); Thomas Piketty, *Capital In the Twenty-First Century* (Cambridge, Massachusetts: The Belknap Press of Harvard University Press, 2014); Geoff Mulgan, *The Locust and the Bee: Predators and Creators in Capitalism's Future* (Princeton: Princeton University Press, 2013); Robert B. Reich, *Saving Capitalism: For the Many, Not the Few* (New York: Vintage Books, 2015); Wolff, *A Century of Wealth In America.*

5. Max Ehrenfreund, "A Majority of Millennials Now Reject Capitalism, Poll Shows," *Washington Post* (April 26, 2016), https://www .washingtonpost.com/news/wonk/wp/2016/04/26/a-majority-of -millennials-now-reject-capitalism-poll-shows/?noredirect=on&utm

_term=.6f9d0fd77226 (also highlighting how a few years earlier, a 2011 poll of the same demographic found that 46 percent had positive views of capitalism and 47 percent had negative views).

6. Mulgan, *The Locust and the Bee*.

7. Joseph E. Stiglitz, *Rewriting the Rules of the American Economy: An Agenda for Growth and Shared Prosperity*, Roosevelt Institute (2015), http://rooseveltinstitute.org/wp-content/uploads/2015/10/Rewriting-the-Rules-Report-Final-Single-Pages.pdf. Stiglitz also published his findings in a book with the same title: Joseph E. Stiglitz, *Rewriting the Rules of the American Economy: An Agenda for Growth and Shared Prosperity* (New York: W. W. Norton & Company, Inc., 2016). In the language of economics, this is called "rent-seeking."

8. Foroohar, *Makers and Takers*; Andrew Ross Sorkin, *Too Big to Fail: The Inside Story of How Wall Street and Washington Fought to Save the Financial System—and Themselves* (New York: Viking, 2009).

9. Stout, *Cultivating Conscience*.

10. Gordon, *The Rise and Fall of American Growth*.

11. In designing a Universal Fund, one policy choice that would need to be made is whether returns from the Fund should count toward income for purposes of determining eligibility for certain government programs, such as Medicare, Social Security Disability, and SNAP (Supplemental Nutrition Assistance Program).

12. Louis Dembitz Brandeis, "What Publicity Can Do," *Harper's Weekly* (December 20, 1913), 10.

13. Associated Press, "Sugar Industry Funded Research to Cast Doubt On Sugars Health Hazards, Report Says," *Los Angeles Times* (September 12, 2016), http://www.latimes.com/science/sciencenow/la-sci-sn-sugar-industry-coverup-20160912-snap-story.html.

14. Ibid.

15. Edward T. Walker, "Grassroots Mobilization, by Corporate America," *New York Times* (August 10, 2012), https://www.nytimes.com/2012/08/11/opinion/grass-roots-mobilization-by-corporate-america.html?mtrref=www.google.com&assetType=opinion&mtrref=www.nytimes.com&gwh=03866D1598500AAA5A1BF5003601F1C7&gwt=pay&assetType=opinion.

16. Transparency International, "Corruption in the USA: The Difference a Year Makes" (December 12, 2017), https://www.transparency.org/news/feature/corruption_in_the_usa_the_difference_a_year_makes.

17. Alexis de Tocqueville, *Democracy in America* (Chicago: University of Chicago Press, 2000) 432.

18. Andrew Kohut, "What Will Become of America's Kids?", Pew Research Center (May 12, 2014), http://www.pewresearch.org/fact-tank/2014/05/12/what-will-become-of-americas-kids.

19. Gordon, *The Rise and Fall of American Growth*.

20. David Sloan Wilson and Peter Barnes, "How to Construct a New Invisible Hand: A Conversation with Peter Barnes," Evonomics (March 3, 2018), http://evonomics.com/new-invisible-hand-conversation-peter -barnes-david-sloan-wilson.

21. David Graeber, *Debt: The First 5,000 Years* (Brooklyn, NY: Melville House Publishing, 2011), 66, 59–69, 136.

22. Ibid., 59, 63.

Chapter 7

1. Kurt Vonnegut Jr., "Harrison Bergeron," *Magazine of Fantasy and Science Fiction* (October 1961).

2. Pew Charitable Trusts, *Moving On Up: Why Do Some Americans Leave the Bottom of the Economic Ladder, but Not Others?* (November 1, 2013), http://www.pewtrusts.org/~/media/assets/2013/11/01/ movingonuppdf.pdf. ("One of the hallmarks of the American Dream is equal opportunity: the belief that anyone who works hard and plays by the rules can achieve economic success.")

3. Stiglitz, *The Price of Inequality.*

4. Horatio Alger Jr. was an American writer best known for his "rags to riches" stories.

5. Taxpayers for Common Sense, "Fact Sheet: Federal Subsidies for Corn Ethanol and Other Corn-Based Biofuels," (June 15, 2015) https://www .taxpayer.net/energy-natural-resources/federal-subsidies-corn -ethanol-corn-based-biofuels.

6. Yussuf Saloojee and Elif Dagli, "Tobacco Industry Tactics for Resisting Public Policy on Health," *Bulletin of the World Health Organization* 78 (2000): 902.

7. Warren E. Buffett, "Stop Coddling the Super-Rich," *New York Times* (August 14, 2011), https://www.nytimes.com/2011/08/15/opinion /stop-coddling-the-super-rich.html?mtrref=www.google.com&gwh =CBA96E947ED4F83CE7BB7B92BAD1848F&gwt=pay&assetType =opinion.

8. Alexis de Tocqueville, *Democracy in America* 489.

9. Robert D. Putnam, *Bowling Alone: The Collapse and Revival of American Community* (New York: Simon & Schuster Paperbacks, 2000).

10. Aaron Smith, "Civic Engagement in the Digital Age," Pew Research Center (April 25, 2013), http://www.pewinternet.org/2013/04/25/civic -engagement-in-the-digital-age-2.

Chapter 8

1. Piketty, *Capital In the Twenty-First Century*; Stiglitz, *The Price of Inequality*; Chris Hughes, *Fair Shot: Rethinking Inequality and How We Earn* (New York: St. Martin's Press, 2018).

2. "The Rich, the Poor, and the Growing Gap Between Them," *The Economist* (June 15, 2006), https://www.economist.com/node/7055911; Moses Naim, "The Problem with Piketty's Inequality Formula," *The Atlantic* (May 27, 2014), https://www.theatlantic.com/international /archive/2014/05/the-problem-with-pikettysinequality-formula /371653/; Jesse A. Myerson, "Five Economic Reforms Millennials Should Be Fighting For," *Rolling Stone* (January 3, 2014), https://www .rollingstone.com/politics/politics-news/five-economic -reforms-millennials-should-be-fighting-for-102489.

3. Matt Egan, "Record Inequality: The Top 1% Controls 38.6% of America's Wealth," CNN Money (September 27, 2017), https://money .cnn.com/2017/09/27/news/economy/inequality-record-top-1-percent -wealth/index.html ("What factors were driving Americans' financial insecurity? The ultimate culprit was wage stagnation, occurring now for over 40 years."); Wolff, *A Century of Wealth In America*, 679.

4. Egan, "Record Inequality" (citing changes in US family finances from 2013 to 2016); "Changes in U.S. Family Finances from 2013 to 2016: Evidence from the Survey of Consumer Finances," *Federal Reserve Bulletin*, vol. 103, no. 3, September 2017, https://www.federalreserve. gov/publications/files/scf17.pdf). See also Wolff, *A Century of Wealth In America*, 644 ("Virtually all the growth in (marketable) wealth between 1983 and 2013 accrued to the top 20% of households . . . Indeed, the bottom 40% of households saw their wealth decline in absolute terms.")

5. Wolff, *A Century of Wealth In America*, 55.

6. We discuss top 10 percent wealth holders in chapter 1. Saez and Zucman discuss the top .01 percent in Emmanuel Saez and Gabriel Zucman, "Wealth Inequality in the United States Since 1913: Evidence from Capitalized Income Tax Data," *Quarterly Journal of Economics* 131 (2016): 519–520.

7. Semuels, "Poor at 20, Poor for Life."

8. Wolff, *A Century of Wealth In America*, 103, table 3.7 (in 2001, 52 percent of households owned stock directly or indirectly; this figure has varied from 32 percent to 46 percent from 1989 to 2013), 123, table 3.11b; (the top 1 percent of wealth holders own 50 percent of all stocks and mutual funds; the top decile owns 91 percent), 103, table 3.7.

9. Oxfam International, "An Economy for the 99%: It's Time to Build a Human Economy That Benefits Everyone, Not Just the Privileged Few," Oxfam briefing paper (January 2017), https://www.oxfam.org/sites /www.oxfam.org/files/file_attachments/bp-economy-for-99-percent -160117-en.pdf.

10. Pew Charitable Trusts, *Moving On Up*; Wolff, *A Century of Wealth In America*, 529 ("households headed by people younger than 25 had remarkably high asset poverty rates—for example, in 2001 more than 72% did not have net worth or liquid assets sufficient to support poverty line consumption for a three-month period").

11. Semuels, "Poor at 20, Poor for Life."

12. Sarah Sattelmeyer, Sheida Elmi, and Joanna Biernacka-Lievestro, "Typical Family Income Improved in 2016—but Financial Stability Remained Elusive," Pew Charitable Trusts (October 2, 2017), http://www.pewtrusts.org/en/research-and-analysis/analysis/2017/10/02/typical-family-income-improved-in-2016-but-financial-stability-remained-elusive.

13. Ibid.

14. Pew Charitable Trusts, "The Role of Emergency Savings in Family Financial Security: What Resources Do Families Have for Financial Emergencies?" (November 2015), http://www.pewtrusts.org/~/media/assets/2015/11/emergencysavingsreportnov2015.pdf?la=en; Erin Currier and Sheida Elmi, "The Racial Wealth Gap and Today's American Dream: Data Suggest Dramatic Differences in Financial Well-Being by Race," Pew Charitable Trusts (February 16, 2018), http://www.pewtrusts.org/en/research-and-analysis/analysis/2018/02/16/the-racial-wealth-gap-and-todays-american-dream.

15. Raj Chetty et al., "The Association Between Income and Life Expectancy in the United States, 2001–2014."

16. See Katie Rogers, "Life Expectancy In the U.S. Declines Slightly, and Researchers Are Puzzled," *New York Times* (December 8, 2016), https://www.nytimes.com/2016/12/08/health/life-expectancy-us-declines.html.

17. Julia Belluz, "What the Dip In U.S. Life Expectancy Is Really About: Inequality," Vox (January 9, 2018), https://www.vox.com/science-and-health/2018/1/9/16860994/life-expectancy-us-income-inequality.

18. Wolff, *A Century of Wealth In America*, 400–401 (from 1983 to 2013, the median wealth of single males almost doubled while the median wealth of single women with children fell by a 93 percent, reaching $500 in 2013), 423; ("households headed by people younger than 25 had remarkably high asset poverty rates—for example, in 2001 more than 72% did not have net worth or liquid assets sufficient to support poverty line consumption for a three-month period"), 529; Currier and Elmi, "The Racial Wealth Gap and Today's American Dream"; "The Role of Emergency Savings in Family Financial Security: What Resources Do Families Have for Financial Emergencies?" (in 2014, the typical white household had enough liquid assets to replace thirty-one days of income, where the typical black household had just five days' worth); Pew Charitable Trusts, "Retirement Security Across Generations: Are Americans Prepared for Their Golden Years?", (May 2013), http://www.pewtrusts.org/~/media/legacy/uploadedfiles/pcs_assets/2013/empretirementv4051013finalforwebpdf.pdf?la=en ("early boomers may be the last cohort on track to retire with enough savings and assets to maintain their financial security through their golden years").

19. "The Hollowing of the American Middle Class," Pew Research Center, Social & Demographic Trends (December 9, 2013),

http://www.pewsocialtrends.org/2015/12/09/1-the-hollowing-of-the
-american-middle-class.

20. Federico Cingano, "Trends In Income Inequality and Its Impact On
    Economic Growth," *OECD Social, Employment, and Migration Working
    Papers*, no. 163 (2014), 11–12, 15, 18. A 2015 study similarly concluded
    that raising the income share of the top 20 percent by one percentage
    point would reduce GDP growth by .08 percentage points over five years.
    Era Dabla-Norris, Kalpana Kochhar, Nujin Suphaphiphat, Frantisek
    Ricka, and Evridiki Tsounta, *Causes and Consequences of Income
    Inequality: A Global Perspective*, IMF Staff Discussion Note (June 2015),
    https://www.imf.org/external/pubs/ft/sdn/2015/sdn1513.pdf.

21. Douglas Rushkoff, *Throwing Rocks at the Google Bus: How Growth
    Became the Enemy of Prosperity* (New York: Portfolio/Penguin, 2015).

22. Alberto Gallo, "How the American Dream Turned Into Greed and
    Inequality," World Economic Forum (November 9, 2017),
    https://www.weforum.org/agenda/2017/11/the-pursuit-of-happiness
    -how-the-american-dream-turned-into-greed-and-inequality.

23. Nick Hauner, "The Pitchforks Are Coming . . . for Us Plutocrats,"
    Politico (July/August 2014), https://www.politico.com/magazine/story
    /2014/06/the-pitchforks-are-coming-for-us-plutocrats-108014; Josh
    Hoxie, "How to Redistribute Wealth—Without Guillotine," *The
    American Prospect* (April 28, 2016), http://prospect.org/article/how
    -redistribute-wealth—without-guillotine.

24. Barb Darrow, "The Bright Side of Job- Killing Automation," *Fortune*
    (April 5, 2017), http://fortune.com/2017/04/05/jobs-automation
    -artificial-intelligence-robotics.

25. Paul Davidson, "Automation Could Kill 73 Million U.S. Jobs By 2030,"
    USA Today (November 29, 2017), https://www.usatoday.com/story/
    money/2017/11/29/automation-could-kill-73-million-u-s-jobs-2030
    /899878001.

26. Kimiko de Freytas-Tamura, "What's Next for Humanity: Automation,
    New Morality, and a 'Global Useless Class,'" *New York Times* (March 19,
    2018), https://www.nytimes.com/2018/03/19/world/europe/yuval-noah
    -harari-future-tech.html. Harari explores this idea further in Yuval
    Noah Harari, *Homo Deus: A Brief History of Tomorrow* (New York:
    Harper/HarperCollins, 2017). An excellent discussion of how
    automation will eliminate even "expert" jobs can be found in Richard
    Susskind and Daniel Susskind, *The Future of the Professions: How
    Technology Will Transform the Work of Human Experts* (Oxford: Oxford
    University Press, 2015).

27. John Maynard Keynes, "Economic Possibilities for Our Grandchildren,"
    Essays in Persuasion (New York: W. W. Norton & Co., 1963, originally
    published 1930).

28. Marjorie Kelly, *The Divine Right of Capital: Dethroning the Corporate
    Aristocracy* (San Francisco: Berrett-Koehler Publishers, 2003).

29. Martin Gilens, *Affluence and Influence: Economic Inequality and Political Power in America* (Princeton: Princeton University Press; New York: Russell Sage Foundation, 2012).

30. Martin Gilens and Benjamin I. Page, "Testing Theories of American Politics: Elites, Interest Groups, and Average Citizens," *Perspectives on Politics* 12 (2014): 564, 575.

31. Stiglitz, *Rewriting the Rules of the American Economy*; Matt Taibbi, *Griftopia: Bubble Machines, Vampire Squids, and the Long Con That Is Breaking America* (New York: Spiegel & Grau, 2010); Jesse Eisinger, *The Chickenshit Club: Why the Justice Department Fails to Prosecute Executives* (New York: Simon & Schuster, 2017).

32. Matt Egan, "Record Inequality: The Top 1% Controls 38.6% of America's Wealth," CNN Money (September 27, 2017), https://money .cnn .com/2017/09/27/news/economy/inequality-record-top-1-percent -wealth/index.html, citing a Federal Reserve report.

33. Pew Charitable Trusts, "Employer-Sponsored Retirement Plan: Access, Uptake and Savings" (September 2016), http://www.pewtrusts.org/en /research-and-analysis/issue-briefs/2016/09/employer-sponsored -retirement-plan-access-uptake-and-savings.

Chapter 9

1. Andy Stern and Lee Kravitz, *Raising the Floor* (New York: PublicAffairs, 2016); Charles Murray, *In Our Hands: A Plan to Replace the Welfare State* (Washington, DC: AEI Press, 2006); Hughes, *Fair Shot*; Phillipe Van Parijs and Yannick Vanderborght, *Basic Income: A Radical Proposal for a Free Society and a Sane Economy* (Cambridge, MA: Harvard University Press, 2017).

2. Milton Friedman, *Capitalism and Freedom* (Chicago: University of Chicago Press, 1962), 191–194. A selection of recent books on the UBI includes: Guy Standing, *Basic Income: A Guide for the Open-Minded* (New Haven; London: Yale University Press, 2017); Barnes, *With Liberty and Dividends for All*; and Annie Lowrey, *Give People Money: How a Universal Basic Income Would End Poverty, Revolutionize Work, and Remake the World* (London: Ebury Publishing, forthcoming July 2018).

3. Catherine Clifford, "What Billionaires and Business Titans Say About Cash Handouts in 2017 (Hint: lots!)," CNBC (December 28, 2017), https://www.cnbc.com/2017/12/27/what-billionaires-say-about -universal-basic-income-in-2017.html. See also Michael Hiltz, "Conservatives, Liberals, Techies, and Social Activists All Love Universal Basic Income: Has Its Time Come?", *Los Angeles Times* (June 22, 2017), http://www.latimes.com/business/hiltzik/la-fi-hiltzik-ubi -20170625-story.html.

4. On a beta test in Kenya, see Annie Lowrey, "The Future of Not Working," *New York Times Magazine* (February 23, 2017), https://www.nytimes.com/2017/02/23/magazine/universal-income -global-inequality.html. On the Y Combinator project in Oakland, see

Amy Graff, "Silicon Valley's Y Combinator to Give People Up to $1,000 a Month In Latest Basic Income Trial," *SFGATE* (September 21, 2017), https://www.sfgate.com/news/article/basic-income-Y-Combinator -Oakland-money-free-12218570.php.

5. Hughes, *Fair Shot*, 5.

6. In fairness to Charles Murray, he does propose slightly reducing (but not eliminating) the size of the UBI payments to those making more than $60,000 annually. Murray, *In Our Hands*, 8.

7. Ibid., ix.

8. Robert H. Frank, "Let's Try a Basic Income and Public Work," Cato Unbound (August 11, 2014), https://www.cato-unbound.org/2014/08 /11/robert-h-frank/lets-try-basic-income-public-work.

9. Stern and Kravitz, *Raising the Floor*, 215.

10. Barnes, *With Liberty and Dividends for All*, 76. In addition to serving the American value of fairness in the form of people opportunity, citizens' dividend programs are also more consistent with the American value of personal responsibility than UBI proposals because the value of the dividend can change according to the financial performance of the asset on which the dividend is based. It thus does not provide a guaranteed payment, instead requiring its recipients to continue to bear some degree of risk, which they are responsible for dealing with.

11. Van Parijs and Vanderborght, *Basic Income*, 71.

12. Christopher May, *Global Corporations in Global Governance* (New York: Routledge, 2015) 104–105.

13. Van Parijs and Vanderborght, *Basic Income*, 71.

Chapter 10

1. Stout, *Cultivating Conscience*.

2. Albert O. Hirschman, *The Rhetoric of Reaction: Perversity, Futility, Jeopardy* (Cambridge, MA: Harvard University Press, 1991).

Conclusion

1. Robert Pirsig, *Zen and the Art of Motorcycle Maintenance* (New York: Harper Collins Publishers, 1974), 102.

2. CitCap.org is overseen by author Tamara Belinfanti.

Acknowledgments

LYNN AND I CONCEIVED THE IDEA of a Universal Fund while we were drafting a short law review article, "Corporate Governance as Privately-Ordered Public Policy: A Proposal." Every time we presented the article, we received comments and suggestions to improve our proposal, and we presented it multiple times on three different continents.

A number of colleagues and friends helped us think our Universal Fund idea through: from Sid Tarrow to David Ciepley, from Jennifer Hill to Andrea Tina, from Hanoch Dagan to Gerald Torres, from Greg Alexander to Robert Green, and many more.

It felt natural to invite Tamara to join us for the transformation of "Corporate Governance as Privately-Ordered Public Policy: A Proposal" into a book. The book is the result of good teamwork. We set this project as our first priority. Lynn, in particular, put in an incredible effort to be able to finish the book with us. She succeeded, but she left us too early to see the project bear fruit.

I want to thank my coauthors; the whole team who participated in this project, from our publisher, to Matt Morrison, to Andrew McDowell, to Theodore Joseph James; Cornell Law School; and the universities that hosted workshops on "Corporate Governance as Privately-Ordered Public Policy: A Proposal" and on Citizen Capitalism—the Simón Bolívar Andean University, the University of Canterbury, the University of Milan, the University of Otago, and Victoria University of Wellington, just to name a few.

I could not have undertaken this ambitious project without Lynn. And I could not have finished this book without the support of my girlfriend, my aunt, my uncle, my cousin, and, in particular, my mother.

Sergio Gramitto

· · · · ·

This book began as a conversation in summer 2017. Lynn and I had just completed a research paper that offered an alternative way for understanding the nature of corporations, and Lynn and Sergio were working on a law review essay, which at the time was called "Blueprint for a More Democratic Capitalism." Over dinner, Lynn and I spoke about the potential for "Blueprint" to be of interest to a broader audience, and as I pointed out to her the various ways in which the work had implications for broader societal concerns, her eyes lit up. "Oh my goodness, I think we have a book!" she exclaimed. "Will you be one of the authors?" The answer to this question was not an obvious yes. Why? Well, Lynn and I had only recently founded a nonprofit, the Ethical Shareholder Initiative, which we were trying to get off the ground, and a few months earlier Lynn had been diagnosed with cancer. We already had our work cut out for us so to speak, and writing a book was an additional commitment that I was not sure we had the capacity to take on.

But we did. We took it on because we believed in the idea, and we believed this was an idea that could help so many people, both in terms of having a voice in corporate behavior and in getting a supplemental income. For some people, a supplemental income makes no difference in their life choices or outcome, but once we dug into the data we quickly realized that having a supplemental income, whether it be $300, $3,000, or $6,000, could make a meaningful difference in the lives of many people. In addition, as much as our plan is about supplemental incomes, it is also about civic engagement in the corporate sector. As we explain in the book, we view this as a key part of having a fair and open society.

I am grateful to Lynn for having the vision and tenacity to make this book a reality. I first met Lynn eighteen years ago when I was a student in her corporate law class at Harvard Law School. I was pretty sure then that I wanted to be an entertainment lawyer, but somehow Lynn convinced me that corporate law, with all its interconnectedness, networks, and hidden dynamics, was much more fun. And to a large extent, she was right.

I am also not sure that this book could have been written without the incredible support of my family and friends. Thanks to my husband, Greg, for helping me refine my thinking on shareholder value and for always encouraging me to not "only see the sky above [my] well." Thanks to my mother, Edris, for lending her editing skills and grammarian prowess. Thanks to my children, Eleanor, Julian, and Gabby, who gave me the space to write this book and who constantly offered fresh perspectives. As Eleanor announced when she was two years old while making up a story about a pencil: "Well, it all began with the corporation." To this day, I don't know whether this is something I should be proud of. I guess it does depend on one's perspective.

Thank you to my colleagues who read drafts and offered support in numerous ways. Special thanks to my New York Law School family for supporting my work on this book.

Thank you to our publishers at Berrett-Koehler and the entire B-K team, who saw the promise of this book and have worked with us at every step of the way to bring it to fruition. And thank you to Andrew MacDowell and our Brooklyn Strategic LLC team, who immediately got the concept and have worked tirelessly to get the word out.

Unfortunately, Lynn did not live to see this book get published. Instead, she left us with a rich body of work from which we can pay it forward. During my last conversation with Lynn a week before she passed, she simply remarked: "It's about caring, dammit! How hard can that be?"

Hopefully this book offers a road map for how we can take care of the present while paying it forward.

With gratitude,

Tamara Belinfanti

Index

Note: Locators followed by the italicized letter *n* indicate material found in notes.

About the Authors

In Memoriam

Lynn Stout was the Distinguished Professor of Corporate and Business Law, Clarke Business Law Institute, at Cornell Law School. Prior to joining the Cornell faculty, Lynn was the Paul Hastings Distinguished Professor of Corporate and Securities Law at UCLA School of Law, and she also taught  at Harvard Law School, NYU Law School, Georgetown University Law School, and George Washington National Law Center. She was an internationally recognized expert on corporate governance and business ethics who lectured widely and wrote for the *Financial Times*, *New York Times*, and *Wall Street Journal*. She is the author of more than forty books and articles on corporate governance, business ethics, financial regulation, law and economics, and moral behavior. Her previous book, *The Shareholder Value Myth: How Putting Shareholders First Harms Investors, Corporations, and the Public*, sparked a global dialogue on the role of corporations in society, while her prior book, *Cultivating Conscience: How Good Laws Make Good People*, demonstrated how better laws can cultivate unselfish and ethical behavior in many realms, including business and politics.

Lynn was deeply committed to the corporate sector and the belief that given the right laws, business in general and corporations specifically have "enormous potential" to be a positive force for good. She served on the board of governors of the CFA Institute; as an independent trustee and chair of the governance committee for the Eaton Vance family of funds; as a member of the board of advisors for the Aspen Institute's Business and Society Program; as an executive advisor to the Brookings Institution's project on the purpose of the corporation; and as a research fellow for the Gruter Institute for Law and Behavioral Research. Lynn also served as a principal investigator and founder of the UCLA-Sloan Foundation Research Program on Business Organizations; as a member of the American Bar Association's Task Force on the Changing Nature of Board/Shareholder Returns; as a member of the board of directors of the American Law and Economics Association; and as chair of the American Association of Law Schools Section on Business Associations.

Lynn spent her last few months working tirelessly on *Citizen Capitalism*. It was Lynn's hope that this book would be a blueprint for how corporations could help to create a brighter future for all. And it was Lynn's wish that the book be dedicated to "all our children," referring not only to those for whom we are parents or legal guardians, but to all children in both current and future generations to whom Lynn fiercely believed we owe a responsibility.

Lynn passed away on April 16, 2018, after living bravely with cancer for more than a year. After her death, Lynn posthumously received the CFA Institute 2018 award for Leadership in Professional Ethics and Standards of Investment Award, in honor of Daniel J. Forrestal III.

Lynn has left us with a remarkable gift, and for that we are eternally grateful.

Sergio Gramitto is a Visiting Assistant Professor of Law at Cornell Law School, where he also serves as the assistant director of the Clarke Program on Corporations and Society. He studied law at University of Milan, and received a Ph.D. from Bocconi University. Sergio is consistently invited to speak at universities around the world.

Tamara Belinfanti is a Professor of Law at New York Law School, where she teaches in the area of contracts and business law. With over fifteen years of experience in corporate law practice and academia, she has written numerous articles and opinion pieces and is a recognized expert on corporate governance, shareholder engagement, and the proxy advisory industry. In 2013, she was named an Aspen Ideas Festival Scholar for her work on the roles and rights of corporations in the broader societal sphere. Prior to entering academia, she was an associate at Cleary Gottlieb Steen & Hamilton LLP, where she focused on capital markets and debt restructuring work, and served as co-editor of the securities law treatise, *U.S. Regulation of the International Securities and Derivatives Market* (Aspen, 2003). Tamara is a board trustee of the Brooklyn Museum and Saint Ann's School; she sits on the advisory board of the Brooklyn Community Foundation and the Brooklyn Ballet; and she has served on various professional committees such as the New York City Bar Securities Regulation Committee. In 2015, she cofounded (with Lynn Stout) the Ethical Shareholder Initiative, a nonprofit focused on building more sustainable capital markets. She received her Juris Doctor, *cum laude*, from Harvard Law School in 2000.

Berrett–Koehler
Publishers

Berrett-Koehler is an independent publisher dedicated to an ambitious mission: *Connecting people and ideas to create a world that works for all.*

We believe that the solutions to the world's problems will come from all of us, working at all levels: in our organizations, in our society, and in our own lives. Our BK Business books help people make their organizations more humane, democratic, diverse, and effective (we don't think there's any contradiction there). Our BK Currents books offer pathways to creating a more just, equitable, and sustainable society. Our BK Life books help people create positive change in their lives and align their personal practices with their aspirations for a better world.

All of our books are designed to bring people seeking positive change together around the ideas that empower them to see and shape the world in a new way.

And we strive to practice what we preach. At the core of our approach is Stewardship, a deep sense of responsibility to administer the company for the benefit of all of our stakeholder groups including authors, customers, employees, investors, service providers, and the communities and environment around us. Everything we do is built around this and our other key values of quality, partnership, inclusion, and sustainability.

This is why we are both a B-Corporation and a California Benefit Corporation—a certification and a for-profit legal status that require us to adhere to the highest standards for corporate, social, and environmental performance.

We are grateful to our readers, authors, and other friends of the company who consider themselves to be part of the BK Community. We hope that you, too, will join us in our mission.

A BK Currents Book

BK Currents books bring people together to advance social and economic justice, shared prosperity, sustainability, and new solutions for national and global issues. They advocate for systemic change and provide the ideas and tools to solve social problems at their root. So get to it!

To find out more, visit **www.bkconnection.com**.

Berrett–Koehler
Publishers

Connecting people and ideas
to create a world that works for all

Dear Reader,

Thank you for picking up this book and joining our worldwide community of Berrett-Koehler readers. We share ideas that bring positive change into people's lives, organizations, and society.

To welcome you, we'd like to offer you a free e-book. You can pick from among twelve of our bestselling books by entering the promotional code **BKP92E** here: http://www.bkconnection.com/welcome.

When you claim your free e-book, we'll also send you a copy of our e-newsletter, the *BK Communiqué*. Although you're free to unsubscribe, there are many benefits to sticking around. In every issue of our newsletter you'll find

- A free e-book
- Tips from famous authors
- Discounts on spotlight titles
- Hilarious insider publishing news
- A chance to win a prize for answering a riddle

Best of all, our readers tell us, "Your newsletter is the only one I actually read." So claim your gift today, and please stay in touch!

Sincerely,

Charlotte Ashlock
Steward of the BK Website

Questions? Comments? Contact me at bkcommunity@bkpub.com.

MIX
Paper from
responsible sources
FSC® C002589

Certified

Corporation
bcorporation.net